WIN-QUATT

A Brief History of

The Dalles, Oregon

D0047989

By Philip and Linda Klindt

Edited by Widge Johnson & Carolyn Wood

2011 First Edition
2011 2nd Printing
© The Philip Klindt Family

Published by Wasco County Historical Museum, The Dalles, Oregon
http://www.gorgediscovery.org

Printed by B&B Printers, Portland, Oregon
http://www.bbprintsource.com

Cover Design and Typeset by Bonham Design
http://www.benbonham.com

ISBN: 978-0-9657586-3-5

Front Cover Photo: Wasco County Historical Museum
Back Cover Photo: Wasco County Pioneers Association

ACKNOWLEDGEMENTS

The editors would like to thank all those who have helped bring this project to fruition. It has truly been a community effort.

In particular we would like to thank:

1) **Mackenzie Wolfe** for scanning, editing and placement of the photos.

2) **Ben Bonham**, of Bonham Design, for cover design and typesetting.

3) **The Discovery Center** for guidance and publication.

4) Photos provided by:

> The Wasco County Pioneer Association (WPCA)
>
> The Columbia Gorge Discovery Center
> & Wasco County Historical Museum (WCHM)
>
> The Dalles Chronicle
>
> Doug Miller (DM)
>
> John Wood (JW)
>
> Philip Klindt Family (PK)
>
> Maria McNamee (MM)
>
> Clackamas County Historical Society
> & Wasco County Historical Society (CCHS & WCHS)
>
> Dennis Kepler (DK)
>
> Phyllis Forman for photo from the L.C. Dickson collection (LCD)
>
> Victor Wolfe (VW)
>
> Rory Johnson (RJ)
>
> Roxie Pennington (RP)
>
> Carolyn Wood (CW)
>
> Widge Johnson (WJ)

5) **The Klindt Family** for permission to continue working on the book; giving us complete access to paperwork, family photos and family history books.

We also acknowledge the assistance of Lisa Becharas, Dave and Peggy Childs, Ken Karsmizki, Rodger Nichols, Carolyn Purcell, Lucille Torgerson, Carmagene Uhalde, Karl and Jean Vercouteren, and Patrick Wolfe.

CONTENTS

INTRODUCTION

Shortly after purchasing the bookstore in The Dalles, Oregon, Philip and Linda Klindt began receiving requests for history books about the town. Those requests inspired them to begin writing a short, concise history that would be of interest to locals as well as tourists.

Between managing their retail businesses and their tours, the book was worked on rather sporadically; adding part of a chapter here, drawing arrows to a possible addition there. Research was mostly compiled by Linda, at night, using many of the rare books from her store.

Unfortunately, and quite unexpectedly, Linda passed away in 2000 at the age of 59, and for the next few years the book was literally shelved.

In 2004, we found Linda's copy of the book and suggested to Philip that he begin working on it again. Several years later, we typed up the manuscript, offering to help recreate the bibliography and fill in the blanks. The project was back on track.

In 2008, Philip was diagnosed with cancer which he battled for almost two years. Chapter revisions, made at his direction, were read to him about two months prior to his passing in 2010. The original text written by Philip and Linda has been edited as little as possible.

Widge Johnson and Carolyn Wood,
long time friends and employees

Linda & Philip Klindt on vacation.   PK

IN THE BEGINNING...

"Long before the Indian had any knowledge of the white men this place (the present location of The Dalles), was called Win-quatt, signifying a place encircled or surrounded by a bold cliff of rocks....The Wasco tribe were the owners of this country, and the village of Win-quatt was their headquarters", according to William C. McKay, from an address to the Ladies' Aid Society of the Congregational Church at The Dalles, May 18, 1869. [1]

WCHM

The Dalles (les dalles in French) was named by French-Canadian fur traders for the many small stone islands through which the river gushed at the Long and Short Narrows east of The Dalles. In French, the name means flagstones

WCHM

and was first mentioned in the notes of the fur trader Franchere in 1814. Many travelers used The Dalles to refer to the entire area of the narrows and rapids east of the bend of the river. The area is now covered by the waters of Celilo Lake, created by The Dalles Dam. The term dalles was also used by the French-Canadian voyageurs to signify the areas where rapidly running waters were constricted between rock walls. In the case of The Dalles, the descriptive term became a proper name.

The Dalles, population 13,006 in 2010, is the county seat of Wasco County. It serves as a commercial center for a population of about 85,000, which includes the neighboring counties. It is located on the Columbia River at the base of a large horseshoe-shaped bend in the river.

The best place to view the town and river is from Kelly Viewpoint at Sorosis Park Overlook, high above the town on Scenic Drive. For a different perspective, a spectacular view of the city, with Mt. Hood in the background, can be had on a clear day from the Washington side of the Columbia River.

Mt. Adams in Washington State from Scenic Drive in Oregon.   WJ

The basin in which The Dalles is located is the only site for miles, east or west, where a large community with easy access to the river could develop. Here the land slopes gently up from the river in a series of benches, and thus the town grew from the river south, up the hill.

"The Dalles is one of the most remarkable places on the Columbia. The river here is compressed into a narrow channel, three hundred feet wide, and half a mile long; the walls are perpendicular, flat on top, and composed of basalt; the river forms an elbow, being situated in an amphitheater extending several miles to the northwest and closed in by a high basaltic wall." [2]

The site is also advantageous because of the abundance of water. The basin is bounded on the east by two creeks; Three-Mile Creek and Eight Mile/Fifteen Mile Creek. These creeks were named for their length as they ran south from The Dalles. It is bordered on the west by two creeks; Mill Creek and Chenoweth Creek. Of the many springs in the basin, one, Amotan Springs, became the site of the Methodist mission established in 1838. The Dalles Wahtonka High School is now located on part of this site, and the water from the spring is still used to keep the school grounds green during hot dry summers.

The first written mention of The Narrows (The Dalles) area is in the journals of Lewis and Clark from 1805. On October 25-27, they camped at Rock Fort Camp near the mouth of Mill Creek, which the natives called Que-nett, meaning salmon trout.

After 10,000 years of Native American trade, the area became a hub for fur traders, missionary work, early migrations, the military, and in the 1860s a booming staging area for the gold miners headed for Central Oregon and Idaho. The first post office was established in 1851, with the name being simply Dalles. In 1853, the early community was called Wascopam. The city was incorporated in 1857 and finally in 1860 became The Dalles City. The city itself was officially called Dalles City until changed to City of The Dalles in 1966.

1   F.A. Shaver, *History of Central Oregon Embracing Wasco, Sherman, Gilliam, Wheeler, Crook, Lake and Klamath Counties*, (Spokane, WA: Western Historical Publishing Co., 1905) pp.86-87.

2   Ibid., p. 89.

GEOLOGY AND LANDSCAPE

Much of the history of The Dalles is connected with its unique location and landscape. The town is located on the western edge of the Eastern Oregon plateau on the Columbia River – the Great River of the West – where it begins to cut a gorge through the Cascade Mountains. Just to the east of the present city were the rapids, narrows, and falls which were a danger to travelers and a fertile fishing ground for the Native Americans. The river was also the primary transportation route through the 19th Century: one either walked or took the river.

When the North American continent began to shift westward some 200 million years ago, the land that is now Washington and Oregon was covered by the waters of a great bay of the Pacific Ocean. Water lapped at the foothills of

Aerial view of Celilo Falls in the Columbia River.   DM

the Blue and Wallowa Mountains, now the border between Oregon and Idaho. The basaltic bedrock of the ocean floor slid beneath the continental plate, sinking toward the molten interior, melted, and re-emerged on the surface as volcanoes. Traces of these ancient volcanoes can still be located in Eastern Oregon.

Millions of years passed as dinosaurs wandered the earth, flourished, then disappeared, and the continent continued its north-westerly drift.

About 30 million years ago, the pattern shifted, a stable land shelf was created, and a string of volcanoes – the present Cascade Range – emerged spectacularly and explosively, sending rivers of molten rock surging into Central Oregon and blanketing the region with clouds of ash, leaving a layer up to 1,000 feet thick in places. This burst of activity lasted about 10 million years, and converted what was left of the great bay into an inland sea. Later, new outpourings in Central and Eastern Oregon produced

Mt. St. Helens erupted May 18th, 1980   WIKI

incredible floods of basalt covering thousands of square miles, filling in what was left of the old inland sea. For the first time most of Oregon was dry land: a volcanic plateau, drained by the ancestral Columbia and other rivers.

River Channel   WCHM

The great Ice Age, with its immense glaciers alternately advancing and retreating, shaped the present Columbia Gorge. The series of great floods at the end of the Ice Age (16,000 to 12,000 B.C.) sculpted the landscape. According to geologists, the advances of the ice sheet from Canada blocked the rivers at least 40 times, and formed ice dams up to 2,000 feet high, creating huge lakes to the east. Probably the last and greatest was a dam formed on the Clark Fork of the Columbia River; it created a 3,000 square mile lake which extended 250 miles into Montana. When the water undermined the ice dam, it was swept away within hours, and the Bretz [1] Flood resulted, sending a wall of water across Idaho, Washington, and Oregon – an estimated 380 cubic miles of water poured out, about 10 times the combined flow of all the rivers of the world, or 60 times the flow of the Amazon, carving out the soft silt and basalt in just a few weeks. The flood crested at The Dalles at about 1,000 feet, with water backed up the valleys of the surrounding creeks; rocks deposited by the flood have been found at the 980 foot elevation of Fifteen Mile Creek.

It topped the Mayer Park Overlook at Rowena, and scrubbed the sides of the Columbia River Gorge, leaving the sheer bluffs and the beautiful waterfalls that we now know.[2] This is also called the Spokane or Missoula flood. In addition, the power of the flood removed great areas of silt and fine sand deposited by earlier glaciers and cut

Klickitat Hills, Washington, across the Columbia River.   WJ

into the underlying basalt - to some 225 feet below sea level in the Big Bend area of the river at The Dalles.

The last of the great floods left the Columbia River Gorge much like it is today. The community of The Dalles developed at the western edge of the old inland sea at the eastern entrance to the Columbia River Gorge. At Rowena, about seven miles west of the city, are the steep bluffs which stopped nearly all land travel westward before the railroad came, forcing most travelers to go down river by water.

Terracing created by ancient floods, still seen today.   WJ

---

1   Named for J. Harlen Bretz, Professor of Geology at the University of Chicago, who first developed the theory of the floods.

2   John Eliot Allen, *The Magnificent Gateway: A Geology of the Columbia River Gorge,* (Forrest Grove, OR.: Timber Press Inc., July 1, 1979), pp. 49-50.

THE LEGEND OF WASCO

"Wasco, like all our original names, has its peculiar origin. Tradition tells us that once upon a time a young man's wife died, leaving two bright, helpless little children, whose only care and succor was found in the love of their grief-stricken father; their continued cries for their forever departed mother caused the children's remaining parent to try all manner of means for the quieting of their grief; so one day he, with a heart full of sadness, while out with his little ones on a hillside for a walk, found a piece of an elk-horn, and with his flint knife cut the string from one of his moccasins and tied a broken flint to it, and after quenching his thirst at a beautiful spring of sparkling cold water (this spring is known as Wasco spring today), sat down beside it on a large rock and began pecking small holes in it, which so amused his loved ones he concluded to make three in a row, making the center one as large as a basin, which represented to them three alone in the world. His relatives, observing the devotion and

Petroglyphs at Horsethief Lake in Washington State.   WJ

attachment for these helpless ones, estranged themselves from him as it was not in accord with their old traditions, and cut him off from their associations, which, with their barbarous habits, forced him to seek refuge away from the home of his childhood. So he took his skin robes, made them in a roll, tied up his war clubs and spears, and set his face with his little darlings toward the Shin-ni-na klath —mountain of the setting sun —

"So he journeyed westward, westward, passed the mountains of the prairie to the kingdom of the west wind. Where he found himself in a land he called Win-quatt, because the new home was walled in by high rocky cliffs. This was the original which we now call The Dalles. Such was the origin from whence sprang into existence the once powerful tribe of Indians known today as the Wascos signifying makers of basins, or more literally, horn basins." [1]

---

1   Shaver, p. 85.

NATIVE AMERICANS

By the time Lewis and Clark came through The Dalles area in 1805, the Native Americans had been here for 11,000 years, and perhaps before that; if so, any traces of their presence would have been wiped out by the great floods at the end of the Ice Age.

The Dalles basin was important to many groups of natives for hundreds of miles around because of the salmon fishing on the Columbia River (N'chiwana, in Sahaptin). From May to October the various species of salmon would migrate upstream to spawn. The Narrows at The Dalles and Celilo Falls, further east, provided a natural fishing ground for the natives who came here each year for the salmon runs. Win-quatt (the Wasco Indian term for The Dalles) became a setting for annual gatherings which included trade, games and gambling, the settling of disputes, and fishing. The countryside nearby was also rich in game, huckleberries, camas root, acorns, and other foods important to their diet. Food was so plentiful that the natives found it amusing that the first missionaries cultivated various food crops when there was such abundance available without additional labor.

Lewis and Clark spent a great deal of time visiting the villages and talking with the Indians. Just above the Long Narrows they describe a village of 21 houses, "which are the first wooden building we have seen since leaving Illinois

Celilo Falls on the Columbia River, OR.   JW

country".[1] These were pit houses, dug into the ground about 6 feet, with split timber walls and timber rafters, covered with a roof of white cedar.

A later explorer, Commander Charles Wilkes, in his report on his expedition of 1841, wrote a detailed description of the Indian way of life, very little changed from that described by Lewis and Clark 35 years earlier:

"The men are engaged in fishing . . ... On the women falls all the work of skinning, cleaning, and drying the fish for their winter stores. So soon as the fish are caught they are laid for a few hours on the rocks, in the hot sun, which permits the skin to be taken off with greater ease; the flesh is then stripped off the bones, mashed and pounded as fine as possible; it is then spread out on mats and placed upon frames to dry in the sun and wind, which effectively cures it. Indeed, it is said that meat of any kind cured in this climate never becomes putrid. Three or four days are sufficient to dry a large

Fishing at Celilo Falls   WCHM

matful, four inches deep. The cured fish is then pounded into a large basket, which will contain about 80 pounds; put up in this way will last for years."

"The hearts, and offal of the salmon they string on sticks and roast over a small fire. Fishing here is much after the manner of that at Willamette Falls, except that there is no necessity for planks to stand on, as there are greater conveniences at The Dalles for pursuing the fishery. They use hooks and spears attached to long poles; both the hook and the spear are made to unship readily, and are attached to the pole by a line four or five feet below its upper end. If the hook were made permanently fast to the end of the pole it would be likely to break, and the large fish would be much more difficult to take. The Indians are seen standing along the walls of the canal in great numbers, fishing, and it is not uncommon for them to take twenty or twenty-five salmon in an hour. When the river is at its greatest height the water in the canals is about three feet below the top of the banks."

Wilkes goes on to say: *"The number of Indians within The Dalles mission is reckoned at about two thousand.….They frequent the three great salmon fisheries of the Columbia, The Dalles, Cascades, and Chutes, and a few were found at a salmon fishery about twenty-five miles up the Deschutes river. The season for fishing*

Along the Columbia River, near The Dalles   WCHM

salmon which is the chief article of food in this country, lasts during five months, from May to September. The country also furnishes quantities of berries, nuts, roots and game, consisting of bear, elk, and deer;.…

After the fishing and trading season is over, they retire to their villages and pass the rest of the year in inactivity, consuming the food supplied by the labors of the preceding summer, and as the season for fishing comes around, they again resort to the fisheries. This is the ordinary course of life among these Indians.….." [2]

The area of The Dalles was the dividing line between two great ethnic and linguistic groups of Native Americans. The Wascos and the Wishrams, who lived below the Narrows and along the Columbia down to its mouth, belong to the Chinookan language family, while the Klickitats, Yakimas, Tyghs, and Teninos living to the east, north and south belonged to the Sahaptin language family. Among the various tribes of Native Americans and whites a trade jargon developed; it was a blend of English, French, Chinook,

Boat on the Columbia   WCHM and other Indian languages, and was also known as Chinook. Philip Klindt's grandfather, Walter Klindt, still used this language with Native Americans in the 1940s.

Lewis and Clark noted with surprise that people living not more than 6 miles apart were separated by a broad distinction of language, each unintelligible to the other.

The coming of the white traders and settlers brought diseases that the Indians had no defenses against. Even before Lewis and Clark, a smallpox epidemic swept through the tribes of the lower Columbia, wiping out perhaps half the population. Again in 1829-30, a second epidemic, a "cold sick", which is now generally believed to have been malaria (or perhaps Asian flu), spread from Fort Vancouver and devastated the population. The trader-explorer Peter Skene Ogden experienced the epidemic at Fort Vancouver, where for twenty days two people nursed the entire garrison. The supply ship, which had just arrived from London, had only one man up and about. A month later Ogden set off to see how the Indians had made out. Ogden's biographer writes:

"The nearest Indian village, of about sixty families, was on a point of land a mile down river, almost within earshot of the fort. But when Ogden approached, instead of the usual sounds of adult activity and the voices of children, there was dead silence; and there was no sign of life. Landing, Ogden found no living human being, only the torn and rotting corpses of Indians of all ages. Some were lying in the shallow water, others at its edge. Ignoring Dr. McLaughlin's common-sense instructions, the Indians had relied on their own method of treating a fever by plunging into cold water; and they had made death unanimous.

Fearing that so many unburied dead would cause another pestilence, Ogden set about disposing of them by the "most purifying of all elements". He and his retching men collected the corpses into heaps and set fire to the point of woods. Almost immediately a new touch of horror was added by human cries. The burial party searched through smoke and brush and were in time to rescue an emaciated old man whose sleep had been disturbed by the fire. He was the last survivor of a village farther down the Columbia; and he had dragged himself up here only to find another village of the dead. Far gone with illness and neglect, he died the next day."[3]

The Reverend Samuel Parker wrote in 1836: *"I have found the Indian population in the lower country - below the falls of the Columbia - far less than I expected, or what it was when Lewis and Clark made their tour. Since the year 1829 probably seven-eights[sic] - if not, as Dr. McLoughlin believes, nine-tenths - have been swept away by disease. So many and so sudden were the deaths which occurred that the shores were strewed with the unburied dead. Whole, and large, villages were depopulated, and some entire tribes have disappeared; but where there were any remaining persons they united with other tribes. This great mortality extended not only from the vicinity of the Cascades to the shores of the Pacific but far north and south."[4]*

In 1853 a smallpox epidemic hit the Wishrams at the Narrows; 150 died. Knowledge of the disease spread among the other tribes and kept them from coming during the summer fishing and trading season - thus ending the traditional trade mart at The Dalles.

Nearly all of the traditional Indian fishing grounds are now lying under the waters of Lake Celilo, behind The Dalles Dam. Much of the

traditional way of life has passed as has access to much of their art and artifacts. Before the waters of the lake inundated the area, archeologists from the Oregon Archeological Society, under supervision of the University of Washington, excavated the site known as Wakemap Mound, an elevated area on the Washington side of the river spotted

Indian settlement near The Dalles, OR. 1900.   RN

by Lewis and Clark in 1805: "A mound about 30 feet above the common level, which has some remains of houses on it, and bears every appearance of being artificial." Here artifacts going back at least 10,000 years were found. But across the river on the Oregon side, at a location at the Five Mile locks site, also called, The Roadcut Site (because the road builders got there before the archeologists), Dr. L.A. Cressman found a long-occupied village site, with evidence that it had been occupied for much longer than the village on the north side of the river.

Greatly diminished and overwhelmed by the power of the white population, the various remnants of tribes of the river and Warm Springs area signed a treaty with the American government in the summer of 1855. This treaty guaranteed to the Indians the fishing rights on the Columbia and Deschutes Rivers, which of course they had possessed from time immemorial, and relegated these tribes to life on the Warm Springs Reservation.

According to Anita Drake, local historian, "Contrary to popular belief, the 1855 treaty was not signed at the location which, until recently, was known as Treaty Oak. It was signed 'at the crossing' of the Creek now called Three-Mile. The oak tree known as Treaty Oak, located in the Nielsen cherry orchard on Mill Creek, was the original Council Oak, where Indians held their council meetings. A copy of the treaty was placed in a crotch of the tree." The tree unfortunately, had slowly died through the years and was taken down in 1987, thereby erasing the explicit commemoration of this Indian council site location.

In the vicinity of the Narrows, at least 10,000-11,000 years old, based on carbon dating of artifacts left behind, was a treasure-trove of Indian art in the form of pictographs and petroglyphs cut into the rocks overlooking the

Tsagaglalal, or She Who Watches, near Horsethief Lake, Washington   WJ

river. Some of these were moved to a higher elevation by the Army Corps of Engineers before the area was flooded.

For many years these were on display at The Dalles Dam, but are now displayed at Columbia Hills State Park in Washington State. The most famous of the petroglyphs, Tsagaglalal, or She Who Watches, is still in its natural location above the Horsethief Lake. Due to recent problems with vandalism, the trail to the petroglyphs is now closed in the winter, and accessible at other times only by advance permission of the State Park, and only when accompanied by a guide.

1   Shaver, p.85.

2   Commander Wilkes, *Narrative of the United States Exploring Expedition, During The Years 1838, 1839, 1840, 1841, 1842,* (NY: G.P. Putnam and Co., 1856), pp. 383-386.

3   Archie Binns, *Peter Skene Ogden: Fur Trader,* (Portland, OR: Binford & Mort Pub., 1967), p. 238.

4   Rev. Samuel Parker, *Journal of an Exploring Tour Beyond The Rocky Mountains,* (Hudson, WI: Ross & Haines, 1967), p. 41.

5

LEWIS AND CLARK

The mouth of the Columbia, the Great River of the West, had been discovered by Captain Robert Gray, a fur trader seeking to do business with the Indians. In May, 1792, Gray crossed the bar of the river in his ship, the *Columbia Redidiva* and named the river after the ship. But Gray was not an explorer; as one historian stated, "*he was a fur trader and any exploration he made was to find unspoiled Indians eager to exchange furs for beads and bright bits of cloth and metal.*"[1] It was left to Lt. William Broughton, who was sailing with Captain Vancouver, to explore the river further. Later in the summer of 1792, Broughton came upstream as far as the Sandy River, east of present-day Portland, and named numerous landmarks, including Mount Hood and Mount Saint Helens. Under orders from Vancouver, he took formal possession of the area for the British.

Mt. Hood, Oregon. Elevation. 11,225 ft.   WIKI

The first recorded presence of the white man in the area of The Dalles is the famous expedition of Meriwether Lewis and William Clark from 1804 to 1806. President Thomas Jefferson ordered the expedition for a number of purposes: to explore the west and to cross the continent to the mouth of the Columbia, to gather data useful to science and commerce, and to establish an American presence in the Northwest. Lewis left Virginia just four days after the announcement of the Louisiana Purchase. The party's route took them up the Missouri, across the Rockies, to the Snake and the Columbia Rivers. Lewis was the official recorder of the expedition. Both his and Clark's journals give detailed descriptions of the landscape, natural history, encounters with Native Americans and their customs, as well as of the difficulties of the journey itself.

At one point the expedition was low on provisions, and bought from the Indians, *"eight small fat dogs, a food to which we are now compelled to have recourse, for the Indians are very unwilling to sell us any of their good fish, which they reserve for the market below."*[2] On October 23, 1805, Lewis says, *"Fortunately, however, the habit of using this animal has completely overcome the repugnance which we felt at first, and dog, if not a favorable dish, is always an acceptable one"*.

Lewis and Clark entered The Dalles area of the Columbia River on October 24, 1805 and their journals give us a detailed description of Celilo Falls, of navigating the Short and Long Narrows, and of the Indian villages they found in the area:

The Short & Long Narrows now covered by The Dalles Dam Lake   WCHM

[Short Narrows] "a channel only 45 yards wide, through which the whole body of the Columbia must press its way. The water, thus forced into so narrow a channel, is thrown into whirls, and swells and boils in every part with the wildest agitation."

Lewis and Clark resolved to pass this in their boats, feeling that the alternative of carrying them over the portage was almost impossible. Clark later wrote that the narrows *"did not appear to be as bad from the top of the rock as when I was in it."*

On October 25, 1805 they passed the Long Narrows: *"The channel for three miles is worn through a hard rough black rock from 50 to 100 yards wide, in which the water swells and boils in a tremendous manner. ….At the end of this channel of three miles, in which the Indians inform us they catch as many salmon as they wish, we reached a deep basin or bend of the river towards the right, near the entrance of which are two rocks. We crossed this basin, which has a quiet and gentle current................"*

The Lewis and Clark expedition spent several days camped at the bend of the Columbia, The Dalles, spending time hunting for game in the hills to the west, and visiting with the Indians.

"At five miles from the large bend we came to the mouth of a creek [interpreted as Mill Creek] 20 yards wide, heading in the range of mountains which runs S.S.W. and

Rock Fort campsite, west of the Union St. underpass   CW

S.W. for a long distance, and discharging a considerable quantity of water; it is called by the Indians Quenett. We halted below it under a high point of rocks on the left; and as it was necessary to make some celestial observations, we formed a camp [named Rock Fort on the return trip in the spring of 1806] on top of the rocks. This situation is perfectly well calculated for defense in case the Indians should incline to attack us, for the rocks form a sort of natural fortification, with the aid of the river and the creek; it is also convenient to hunt along the foot of the mountains to the west and southwest, where there are several species of timber which form fine coverts for game. From this rock the pinnacle of the round mountain covered with snow, which we seen a short distance below the forks of the Columbia, and which we had called the Falls or Timm mountain, is S. 43 W., about 37 miles distant. [Here Clark had written "This is the Mount Hood of Vancouver."] The face of the country on both sides of the river, above and below the falls, is steep, rugged, and rocky, with very small proportion of herbage, and no timber except a few bushes; the hills to the west however, have some scattered pine, white-oak, and other kinds of trees."[3]

Although the Lewis and Clark expedition is the first recorded presence of white men in the Columbia Gorge area, it is evident from their journals that the Indians had met and traded with Europeans before this time.

"We were about setting out when...canoes.....came to visit us. Among these last was an Indian who wore his hair in a cue and had on a round hat and a sailor's jacket, which he said he had obtained from the people below the great rapids, who bought them from the whites..............

.....At a distance of four miles we reached a small village of eight houses under some high rocks on the right [at or near Crate's Point]....We landed and found the houses similar to those we had seen at the great narrows; on entering one of them we

saw a British musket, a cutlass, and several brass tea-kettles, of which they seemed to be very fond." [4]

This evidence of contact should come as no surprise, since the previous century had been one of great exploration and commerce. The Spanish had come up the West Coast, seeking riches and land. They established presidios in California and gave names to various Northwest landmarks, such as Heceta. Russian sailors explored the North Pacific, traveling up the Hoh River on the Washington coast and trading with Indians in Washington. They eventually established a trading base as far south as Fort Ross, in northern California. The British were also active in exploring the coast, seeking the elusive Northwest Passage around the continent. The voyages of Captain Cook, who is credited with discovering the Hawaiian Islands (which he named the Sandwich Islands),

Columbia River Gorge   WIKI

eventually gave impetus to the fur trade with China. His crew, who continued the voyage after Cook was murdered in Hawaii, were amazed to find that the Chinese were enthusiastic buyers of the sea otter skins, which the sailors had bought for a trifling amount. Word of this lucrative trade spread quickly and by 1789, ships of France, Russia, Spain, Britain, and the newly independent United States were in the North Pacific. In addition, British and French trappers and traders came overland from Canada, exploring the waterways and mountains of the area. In fact, Lewis and Clark's interpreter, Sacagawea's husband, Toussaint Charbonneau, was a French-Canadian trapper.

The reports of Meriwether Lewis and the maps and drawings of William Clark stimulated the already great interest in the land.

---

1   Dorothy O. Johansen, *Empire of the Columbia,* (NY: Harper & Row, 1956), p. 58.

2   Nicholas Biddle, *The Journals of the Expedition Under the Command of Capts. Lewis and Clark,* (NY: Heritage Press, 1962), October 10, 1805.

3   Ibid., October 25, 1805.

4   Ibid., October 28, 1805.

6

THE ERA OF EXPLORATION

In 1810-11, John Jacob Astor, together with Canadian partners lured by the promise of a profitable fur trade, made plans to establish a series of trading posts in the Northwest. He sent two expeditions to the mouth of the Columbia. The overland expedition, headed by Wilson Prince Hunt, was to cross by land and locate sites for a chain of posts. A second party was dispatched by ship to set up a trading post on the Columbia. The *Tonguin* reached the west coast in March,

David Thompson's route along the Columbia River.   DK

1811, and chose the site for Fort Astoria. Unfortunately, the ship was destroyed by antagonized natives and all crew members who were still on board were killed.

Three months later, July 14th, 1811, David Thompson, Canadian fur trader and map maker, arrived at the mouth of the Columbia to find it already claimed by Astor. After a week he returned up the Columbia to his winter camp on Canoe River, being the first to traverse the full length of the Columbia River.

The Hunt party, which had started following the route of Lewis and Clark, decided on a more southerly route when they heard of hostile Indians. They crossed the Tetons, and made a grueling and hazardous journey along the Snake, covering much of the distance on foot. The party reached The Dalles in January, 1812.

"[At Umatilla] the toilsome hazardous portion of their journey was at an end. But they had no timber for the manufacture of boats; the Indians were unwilling to sell them canoes. Thus they were compelled to wait until reaching The Dalles before they launched upon the bosom of the stream. In the vicinity of the present Rockland (they had come from Umatilla on the south bank of the river) they had a "hyas wa wa" with the redoubtable Wishram Indians. Sharpened by their location at the confluence of all the ways downstream, these Indians had clearly grasped the fundamental doctrine of civilized trade, to wit: get the greatest return with the least possible outlay. To this end they levied a heavy toll on all unwary travelers.... At first, they endeavored to frighten Mr. Hunt into a liberal "potlatch". Then they represented the great service they had rendered the party in protecting them from the rapacity of other Indians; but finding no ready recognition of their claims save an occasional whiff of the pipe of peace, they gave up in disgust and contented themselves with picking up what little articles might be lying loose. After no little haggling several finely made canoes were procured of these people...." [1]

The Hunt Party arrived at Fort Astoria in February of 1812, only to find trouble there. With the loss of the *Tonquin*, supplies and trading stock were low. In June, a young Robert Stuart set off with a company of men across the continent to report the loss of the ship. Traveling east, Stuart retraced the route taken by the Hunt party the previous year. His party followed the Columbia to Walla Walla, then south to the Umatilla and on into southwest Idaho, following the Snake. When they reached the area of eastern Idaho, they encountered an Indian who had accompanied the westbound Hunt Party in this area. He told them of a short cut across the Rockies - probably *"this was the first definite word of South Pass to reach white ears."* [2] First Stuart detoured north to the area of today's Teton National Park, fearing unfriendly Indians. Later he returned southeast, and on October 22, crossed South Pass, *"the first known traverse of the broad gateway to the West."* [3] Stuart essentially traced the route of the future Oregon Trail. However, the South Pass Route across the Rockies was not to be used, at least intentionally, for another ten years, until the mountain man, Jedediah Smith and his party traveled over it in 1824 on a trapping expedition. [4]

When Stuart arrived in St. Louis, the local newspaper, *The Missouri Gazette* of May 15, 1813, had the following article: *"By information received from these gentlemen, it appears that a journey across the continent of North America might be performed in a wagon, there being no obstruction on the whole route that any person would dare call a mountain in addition its being much the most direct and short one to go from this place to the mouth of the Columbia River. Any future party who may undertake this journey, and are tolerably acquainted with the different places, where*

Celilo Falls on the Columbia River.   WCHM

it would be necessary to lay up a small stock of provisions, would not be impeded, as in all probability they would not meet with an Indian to interrupt their progress...."[5]

In 1812, The Robert Stuart party was accompanied by the French voyageur Gabriel Franchere, who was the first to put into writing the term "the dalles" in referring to the area of the narrows and rapids of the Columbia.

With the War of 1812 impeding supply of Fort Astoria by ship, partners of Astor sold the Pacific Fur Company to the Canadian Northwest Fur Company, thus ending substantial American commercial interests in the Northwest for the next 30 years. Future trading posts were established by the Hudson Bay Company in what is now Washington State, including Fort Nez Perce (Walla Walla), 1826, and Fort Vancouver, 1824, and the British presence was felt. Treaties provided for *"joint occupation"*; in fact the land west of the Rockies was free and open.... *"to the vessels, Citizens and Subjects of the Two Powers."*[6]

Brief mentions are made of an early trading post at The Dalles; however, *The History of Central Oregon*, states only, *"Of the Hudson Bay Company's post at the Dalles there is only meager information concerning the details available. It is certain, however, that this gigantic fur trust and syndicate of speculative English capitalists established a post, or "factory" at this point in 1820, and that James Birnie,[7] a Scotchman and native of Aberdeen, was in charge of the same"*. It apparently existed only a short time, and it is very likely no permanent building was ever erected. [8]

Peter Skene Ogden, explorer, trader and trapper, called The Dalles one of the most dreaded of the rapids. During his 1830 expedition along the Columbia, nine men in his party were lost in the rapids. His description of the event 23 years after the fact is still vivid.

"It was in the summer of 1830 that I arrived at the Dalles on my return to Vancouver....I had a small party of trappers under my command, and having left our horses at Walla Walla, where a crazy boat had been furnished us, we had reached thus far on our descent without an accident of any sort.... The heat was intense; and though the breakfast hour was gone by, the stench of putrefying salmon was so over powering, that I resolved on proceeding a few miles lower down.... Accordingly, the men were directed to push off and prepare for this important event of the day at a spot indicated, while I resolved to saunter downward by land...."

Rushing river   WCHM

"Scarcely had I set out, when the men put forth, and began steering in an oblique direction cross the stream, in order to avoid a string of whirlpools....Suddenly, however, the way of the boat was checkered; so abruptly, too, that the rowers were nearly thrown from their seats. Recovering their equilibrium, they bent to their

oars…but the craft yielded nought to their endeavors. The incipient gyrations of a huge whirlpool at the same instant began to be felt…."

"The vortex was rapidly forming, and the air was filled with a confused murmur…The boat glided, at first slowly, into the whirling vortex; its prow rising fearfully as the pitiless waters hurried it round with increasing velocity…."

"The spot where the boat had disappeared, no longer offered any mark whereby to note the sad catastrophe that had even now occurred there….A few moments more, and the paddles, sitting poles, and various other articles….were cast up in all directions around, while here and there, a struggling victim was discoverable…. One by one they disappeared…. (One of the party miraculously survived by seizing four empty kegs which had been lashed together and floated through the rapids.)" [9]

In 1832 an expedition led by Nathaniel Wyeth came west, hoping to set up a commercial operation dealing in both fur and salmon. Inspired by the enthusiasm of Hall Jackson Kelley, probably the primary propagandist for Oregon settlement in the 1820's and 1830's, Wyeth organized a party of 24 to go to the Willamette Valley. However, by the time they reached the mountains, over half had left the party. Wyeth was forced to cache his trading goods for lack of horses, and arrived in Fort Vancouver nearly destitute. Looking over the Willamette Valley, he wrote, *"I have never seen country of equal beauty except the Kansas country, and I doubt not it will one day sustain a large population."*

Wyeth reached The Dalles on October 14, 1832. Like the travelers before him, he was impressed with the falls and rapids, the awesome power of the river forced through the narrows. He also learned of other Europeans who had preceded them:

"Indians Plenty one chief at whose lodge we stopped a short time gave me some molasses obtained from [the] fort below to eat. He had a large stock of dried fish for the winter 4 tons I should think roots. He was dressed in the English stile Blue frock coat pants & vest comported himself with much dignity enquired my name particularly and repeated it over many times to impress it on his memory his sister was the squaw of an American of the name of Bache who established a post on the river below the great dalles three years ago last fall and who was drowned in them with 11 others the following spring the remains of the fort I saw as also the grave of the woman who died this fall and was buried in great state with sundry articles such as a capeau vest pantaloons shirts &c. … at the foot of the Dalles is an island called the Isle of the Dead on which there are many sepulchers these Indians usually inter their dead on the Islands in the most romantic situations where the souls of the dead can feast themselves with the roar of the mighty an eternal waters which in life time afforded them sustenance and will to all eternity to their posterity." [10]

During his 1834 expedition, Wyeth again camped at The Dalles, this time mentioning only the great gales which kept the party from moving on as fast as possible. The missionary Jason Lee was a member of Wyeth's party at this time.

Lee commented that a hundred or more Indians, *"crowded around us as soon as we arrived and followed us across the portage, and watched all our motions till we embarked.*" Also complaining about being held back by the winds, Lee's attitude can also be seen in the comment that "*our provision is nearly done except flour, but I have no anxious hours, trusting that he who ruleth the wind will provide for us.*" When the Indians brought salmon the next day, he wrote, "*the fount of spiritual blessing is as near us in this western desert as it is to those who dwell in Christendom....*"[11]

---

1   Shaver, p. 28.

2   David Lavender, *Westward Vision: The Story of the Oregon Trail,* (Lincoln, NE: University of Nebraska Press, 1963), p. 161.

3   Ibid., p. 165.

4   Ibid., pp. 182-183.

5   Ibid., p. 166.

6   William Denison Lyman, *The Columbia River: Its History, Its Myths, Its Scenery, Its Commerce,* (Portland, OR: Binford & Mort, 1963), p. 184.

7   James Birnie, who was designated by the editors of History of Central Oregon as the "first inhabitant of The Dalles" died in Cathlamet, WA, at age 69 in 1864.

8   Horace Lyman, *History of Oregon; the Growth of an American State,* (NY: North Pacific Pub. Society, 1903), Vol. II, p. 334.

9   Binns, pp. 234-235.

10   Nathaniel Wyeth, *Journal of Captain Nathaniel J. Wyeth's Expeditions to the Oregon Country, 1831-1836,* (Fairfield, WA: Ye Galleon Press, 1965), p. 29.

11   "Jason Lee Diary", <u>Oregon Historical Quarterly,</u> Vol. 16, No.1. (March, 1915), pp. 258-259.

7

MISSIONARIES

The first interest in establishing a mission at The Dalles came in 1836, when the Whitman party and P.C. Pambrun of the Hudson's Bay post at Walla Walla traveled through the area on their way to and from Fort Vancouver. They did not locate at The Dalles, however, and proceeded up the Columbia to establish the Whitman mission at Waiilatpu (near Walla Walla). Of this trip, W.H. Gray wrote:

"Our mission party, with Captain Pambrun, his two boats loaded, two-thirds of the goods for the mission, on their way up the Columbia River, arrived all safe at The Dalles. Gray took a decided stand in favor of the first location at the point on account of its accessibility and the general inclination of all the Indians in the country to gather at these salmon fisheries; Spalding and Pambrun opposed; Whitman was undecided; Pambrun would not wait to give time to explore nor assist in getting horses for the doctor and Gray to look at the country in view of a location."[1]

The first permanent white settlement in The Dalles was the Methodist mission established in 1838 by Daniel Lee (nephew of Jason Lee, who established the first mission in the Willamette Valley in 1834) and H.K.W. Perkins. They referred to the mission as Wascopam after the Indians who lived here. The mission remained very small until 1840, when three other families joined the first two ministers.

The first log residence was built in early April, 1838, with the assistance of the Indians, near a valuable spring of water. When explorer, T.J. Farnham, visited the mission in 1839, he found several buildings:

Methodist Mission sketch, 1838   WCHM

"The buildings of the mission are a dwelling-house, a house for worship and for school purposes, and a workshop, &c. The first is a log structure 30 by 20 feet, one and a half stories high, shingle roof, and the floors made of plank cut with a whip-saw from the pines of the hills. The lower story is divided into two rooms – the one a dining-room, the other a family apartment of Mr. Perkins and lady. These are lined overhead and at the sides with beautiful rush mats manufactured by the Indians. The upper story is partitioned into six dormitories and a school-room for Indian children; all neatly lined with mats. Underneath is an excellent cellar. The building designed for a house of worship, was being built when I arrived..."[2]

Meetings with the Indians started immediately. The missionaries used the services of an interpreter who spoke the Chinook Jargon, the trade language which had developed for communication among the tribes and later between the Indians and traders. The religious meetings were held among the oaks or under a pine; scattered stones were used as seats for some, while others squatted on the ground. Tradition says that the missionaries delivered their sermons from Pulpit Rock (located at present day Twelfth and Court Streets). Scriptures were read and explained both morning and evening.

In the winter of 1839-40, a wave of religious enthusiasm swept through the Indian population, in the spirit of a revival. Business was laid aside; great groups congregated in the open air, with the high point at a camp meeting in April 1840. Nearly 1200 Indians were present, many professed religion, 150 were

THE LORD'S PRAYER.

Nesika Papa klaksta mitlite kopa Saghalie,
Our Father who lives in the Above,

kloshe mika nem kopa konoway kah.
good thy name over everywhere.

Kloshe spose mika chaco delate Tyee kopa
Good if thou become true Chief over

konoway tillikums. Klosh spose mika
all people. Good if thy

turntum mitlite kopa illahee, kahkwa kopa
mind is on the earth, as in

Saghalie. Potlatch kopa nesika kopa okoke
the Above. Give to us during this

sun nesika muckamuck. Mamook klahowya
day our food. Pity

nesika kopa nesika mesachie mamook,
us for our wickedness,

kahkwa nesika mamook klahowya klaksta
as we pity any

man spose yaka mamook mesachie kopa
man if he does evil to

nesika. Wake mika lolo nesika kopa kah
us Not thou carry us to where

mesachie mitlite ; pe spose mesachie klap
evil is ; but if evil find

nesika, klose mika help nesika toto okoke
us good thou help us conquer that

mesachie. Delate konoway illahee mika
evil. Truly all earth thy

illahee, pe mika hias skokum, pe mika delate
earth, and thou very strong, and thou truly

hias kloshe, kahkwa nesika tikegh konoway
very good, so we wish all

okoke. Kloshe kahkwa.
this. Good so.

Lord's prayer in Chinook Jargon Language   Eels, Myron

baptized, and 400-500 took part in communion. Although the missionaries were ecstatic, a traveler, also a minister, recalled the following exchange:

Easter service, 1929 at Pulpit Rock; located at 12th & Court Streets, The Dalles, OR   WCHM

"We remarked that, in our opinion, most of the religious professions of the natives were from selfish motives. Mr. Perkins thought not; he named one Indian that, he felt certain, was really converted, if there ever was a true conversion. In a short time Daniel Lee, his associate, came in and remarked, "What kind of proposition do you think _____(naming Mr. Perkins' truly converted Indian) has made to me?" Perkins replied: "Perhaps he will perform the work we wished him to do." "No," says Lee, "he says he will pray a whole year if I will give him a shirt and a capote (coat)". This fact shows that the natives who were supposed to be converted to Christianity were making these professions to gain presents from the missionaries."[3] In fact, ten years later, when the mission was abandoned, there were almost no natives who remained Christian.

The first crops were planted in the spring of 1839, although the missionaries' efforts to raise food where nature provided such bounty was treated as a joke by the Indians. Still, a few garden vegetables and a good crop of potatoes were raised and later wheat was grown.[4]

By 1841, when Commander Charles Wilkes, an explorer, visited The Dalles,

Early Town   DM

the mission consisted of two log and board houses *"hewn, sawed, and built by [the missionaries], with a small barn and several outhouses...."*[5] He found that they had raised wheat and potatoes by irrigating with water from the springs and streams nearby. Wilkes was not surprised that the missionaries felt discouraged by the lack of progress they

26

had made in reforming the Indians, since "*the missionaries...consider covetousness as their [the Indians'] prevailing sin, which is exhibited in lying, dishonest traffic, gambling and horse-racing, of which they are extremely fond*." [6]

The Lees left in 1843, and were replaced first by George Gray, then by William Roberts. In charge of the mission during the 1845 migration was the Reverend Alvin F. Waller, who had been assigned there earlier in the year "*to teach the Indians the white man's Christian way of life*." The efforts of the missionaries in Oregon had been supported by the Methodist Church for nearly 10 years, but after 1843, the mission began to serve mainly as a supply station for the Oregon Trail emigrants, putting an immense strain on the Church's finances. In 1847, the mission was sold to Marcus Whitman for $600; he left his 17 year old nephew, Perrin Whitman, in charge. This was fortunate for Perrin, because a few months later, the Whitmans were killed by local natives in Walla Walla. Upon hearing of the massacre, Perrin [7] fled down river, leaving the mission in charge of some friendly Wascos; thus ending the Methodist mission at The Dalles.[8]

Later the Methodist Church tried to claim all the land that had belonged to the mission, but in 1879, a law suit with the City of The Dalles was decided against the Church, on the grounds that it had abandoned the property.

The buildings of the abandoned mission were used briefly by the voluntary military company under Captain H.A.G. Lee. It was originally known as Fort Wascopam. Later it was known as Fort Lee, which became Camp Drum when it was established as a federal military reservation in 1850. In 1853 the name was

Surgeon Quarters at Old Fort Dalles   DM

changed to Fort Drum and in 1855 became Fort Dalles. One of the original buildings, now a museum, still stands at West Fifteenth and Garrison Streets.

After the conclusion of the Indian War of 1847-48, a Catholic mission was established near The Dalles in 1848, under Reverend L. Rosseau, who crossed the plains the year before.

Father Rosseau, it is said, was extremely handsome, and an impressive and eloquent preacher who had much influence with the Indians. The site of the mission was near the present location of the Catholic cemetery, west of town. Father Rosseau was succeeded by Father Mesplie in 1851, who supervised the construction of the mission buildings. On the whole, the Catholics were no more successful at converting the Indians than their Methodist predecessors had been: *"….when [Father Mesplie] asked them to perform the slightest religious duty, they invariably asked, "What will you pay me?" And this reminds us of an incident: A party attended the church one Sunday morning, and were quite highly entertained by hearing the priest preach to the Indians in Chinook, telling them Bible stories……well, very highly dressed, trying to make them understand by these miracles the magnitude of the power of God. But he had to pay them to believe these things so the good father left."* [9]

The first Catholic church was a simple log house without a floor, and lined with mats. The congregation also sat on mats on the floor. Services were in both Latin and Chinook. In 1851, the old mission building burned when the matting caught fire from a candle, and Father Mesplie oversaw the construction of a frame church, a more church-like building with a steeple and a bell out of sawed lumber from the government military sawmill at Ninth Street and Mill Creek Road on the old Methodist mission grounds. By 1861, the Church acquired land closer to the growing city, and built a white church on the corner of Third and Lincoln Streets. The fourth church, St. Peter's, built in 1898, was listed in 1974 on the National Register of Historic Properties and is presently open to the public.

3rd Catholic Church   DM   3rd & 4th Catholic Churches   WCPA

4th Catholic Church under construction   DM

St. Peter's Church & St. Marys Academy, W. 3rd & Lincoln   JW

A Catholic school, which came to be known as St. Mary's Academy, was established in August, 1864, by the Sisters of the Holy Names of Jesus and Mary. It was first located in a small wooden building at Fourth and Lincoln Streets. During the first year, 62 boys and 81 girls were crowded into the building, which contained a grade school and a high school. At that time it was the only high school in Wasco County. Even summer term the first year was a success:

The Dalles Times-Mountaineer of August 4, 1865, reported that 59 boys and 81 girls attended that summer.

A boarding school was added in 1867. The Academy moved to a larger wooden building at Second and Lincoln in 1871, but this building also proved too small. It was moved across the street where it became a residence on Third place. A large, 3-story, brick building was constructed in 1884. This new building had 30 inch thick solid brick walls in the lower portion and survived both fire and flood. During the great flood of 1894, water stood 61 inches deep in the academy, and left a deep layer of mud, requiring massive clean-up. The building itself remained undamaged, *"….the foundations of St. Mary's stood as firm as her principles…,"* as the sisters would say decades later.

In 1956, the Academy moved to new quarters near West Tenth Street and Cherry Heights Road. The teaching staff continued to use the old brick building as a convent until a new one was built near the school. The old building was razed in the spring of 1962.

---

1   Shaver, p. 98.

2   Thomas J. Farnham, *1839 Wagon Train Journal: Travels in the Great Western Prairies…..and the Oregon Territory,* (Monroe, OR: Northwest Interpretive Assoc., 1983), p. 81.

3   Shaver, p. 100.

4   Ibid., p. 99.

5   Ibid., p. 29.

6   Ibid., p. 101.

7   Perrin Whitman did return to the area later to take part in the battles against the Indians, in which he served "with conspicuous bravery".

8   Shaver, p. 100.

9   Ibid., p. 102.

OREGON TRAIL FEVER

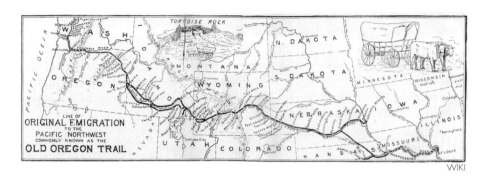

"Then it may be asked, why did such men peril everything – burning their ships behind them, exposing their helpless families to the possibilities of massacres and starvation, braving death – and for what purpose? I am not quite certain that any rational answer will ever be given to that question." [1]

Enthusiasm for Oregon built gradually. The tales of the explorers, reports from the missions, the writings of the fur traders, and the increasing information about the route itself percolated back East. Missionaries had come with their wives. Wagons had made it, first to the Rockies, and then the Marcus Whitman party had made it almost to Fort Walla Walla with two wagons. Actually they had made it only as far as Fort Hall in Idaho. These wagons were cut down to carts which they finally abandoned at Fort Boise but to Easterners' imaginations, this was close enough. Now families could make the trip, and bring their belongings. And there was fertile farm land in the Willamette Valley - rich, dark loam that produced bumper crops and it was free for the taking! (At least that was the hope - a bill was introduced in Congress

Pioneers   WCHM

that proposed making Oregon a territory and guaranteeing land to settlers.) There was no snow to keep a person indoors during the winter. And to people ill with "river fever" in the Mississippi lowlands, the lure of the mild and healthful climate had great appeal. The Willamette Valley was the promised "New Eden".

In addition, the economic panic of 1837 hit Midwest farmers hard, and the depression of 1842 cut even deeper. The slavery issue was also worrisome, with pro-slavery groups becoming restless mobs. For some people the patriotic desire to secure the Northwest for the United States was a motive. And for at least some young men, there was a promise of adventure.

In 1839, the first "real emigration," a group of nineteen, called, "Peoria Party," started out, in an attempt to reach Oregon. However, the effort soon fell apart, although a couple of young men reached the Willamette Valley. One, Robert Shortess wrote letters full of praise to his friends the Applegates. Another, T.J. Farnham, had a book published; however, he himself had become disillusioned, and wrote letters decrying the Northwest.

In 1840 and 1841, small groups made the trek to Oregon, including the mountain men Doc Newell and Joe Meek, who brought the first wagons to Walla Walla in 1840. And in 1842, a total of 112 people left Independence, Missouri, the majority going down the Santa Fe Trail, but a handful made it to the Willamette Valley. In fact, Newell and Meek found the lava boulders and sagebrush tough going, so they discarded the wagon boxes, packing their goods on horses, and continued with just the running gear. They made it to the Whitman mission and on to Fort Walla Walla, leaving what remained of the wagons. Newell returned the next spring, loaded the wagon onto a barge, and floated it down river. He wrote: *this is to be remembered that I Robert Newell was the first who brought wagons across the Rocky Mountains.*[2]

By the year 1843, the year of the Great Migration, the trickle became a torrent. An estimated 875 people made the trip in more than 120 wagons (perhaps as many as 250 started out - estimates vary, since some defected or turned back) with livestock estimated at 2000-5000 head. Only 700 animals reached the Valley. These pioneers were understandably nervous about the journey, but soon

they learned that the famed Dr. Marcus Whitman, who had returned to the East Coast the previous year to plead for continuation of the mission, would accompany the train. The first train was also blessed with

Wagon Train   WCPA   other able leaders:

Jesse Applegate leading the cow column, which traveled behind the main train; Peter Burnett, who later became governor of California, was chosen captain of the train, although Burnett soon asked to be relieved of his position.

Although the emigration of 1843 was the first one of any size, the first with any great numbers of cattle, and the first to bring wagons over several portions of the Trail, it had, according to historian William D. Lyman, *"perhaps the least trouble and misfortune and the most romance and gayety and enthusiasm of any."* Out of the nearly 1000 emigrants, only 8 died before reaching The Dalles, although four more were drowned here.[3]

At Walla Walla, the train diverged: those whose draft animals still had strength traveled the last 125 miles to The Dalles along the south bank of the Columbia River. Others either purchased one of the few 30 foot canoes at Fort Walla Walla, or, like the Applegates, built their own mackinaws (boats with square sterns) by whipsawing driftwood logs into boards. The portages at Celilo and The Dalles were difficult. Two young Applegate cousins, as well as one older man, were drowned coming through the narrows in their boat when its steering pin broke – the cousins were nine years old.

From 1843 to 1845, The Dalles was the end of the overland route of the Oregon Trail. At Rowena, seven miles west of The Dalles, the bluffs closed in on the river, making further passage by wagon impossible. Only single-file tracks went over the mountains, barely passable to cattle and pack animals, but not to emigrants bringing tools and supplies to begin a new life in the

Ezra Meeker, Oregon trail pioneer commemorated the end of the Oregon Trail in 1906 with marker placed at City Park on Union St., The Dalles, OR
DM

Willamette Valley. Here the majority would build large rough rafts on which they could load their wagons and float to the next rapids. There they had to reassemble the wagons and portage around the Cascades, while Indians used a network of ropes to get the rafts through the rapids.

In 1843, and in future years, help came upriver to those who made it to The Dalles. Settlers already in Oregon sent boats and supplies upstream and Dr. John McLoughlin, the Chief Factor (head) of Fort Vancouver, provided much appreciated aid to exhausted emigrants. Unfortunately, some of this aid did not reach the emigrants in the generous spirit in which it had been offered:

"At The Dalles Mission we took to the water - in one of the Hudson's Bay boats which some of our kind hearted, noble free born Americans got from the company for nothing and charged for a wagon and family a damage of from fifty to sixty dollars in cash, or trade in proportion, to be taken to Linnton which takes ten days a trip and five or six families to load. Those who had the cash got down very readily and those who had nothing but cattle had to wait...."[4]

Emigrants arriving at The Dalles were often exhausted from their travels and low on supplies. John C. Fremont, who led an expedition to California via Oregon in 1843, described the many emigrant families: *"their thin and insufficient clothing, bare-headed and bare-footed children attesting to the length of journey, showing not much preparation."*[5]

The mission storehouse rations were mainly potatoes, dried peas, and a limit of eight quarts of flour per family. In some years, the people were so famished that they would eat the food only partially cooked and become seriously ill. The missionaries required payment in cash, or cattle at one-third the value – prices which many emigrants thought were exorbitant, although others realized that the mission was not a supply depot and appreciated the food that was available. It is clear that the missionaries often

Wood Scow, Ella F., at boat landing in The Dalles. Opposite shore shows shoe factory in Dallesport, WA.   WCPA

resented their role in the emigration: for example, they let Stephen Meek know that *"they were appointed by the Mission Board to teach the Indians the word of God, not to minister to the annual hoard of refugees from the states, nor did they run a guide service for those who became lost."*[6] Boatmen would also bring supplies up from the valley, charging eight to ten dollars per hundredweight of flour which had cost them four dollars in the valley. Of course, not all the emigrants had the money to pay. Some preferred to save what little they had to establish themselves in the Willamette Valley. Others lived on roots or salmon they got from the Indians.

Yet, in spite of the difficulties, and the knowledge that the hardest part of the journey remained ahead, there was a feeling of elation: the Eden of the Willamette Valley was within reach - only 135 miles away; nearly 2000 miles of dusty trail was behind them.

In The Dalles, families had a few days respite from travel as they built rafts or prepared their belongings to be shipped by water. The Dalles was somewhat of a haven - wagons did not have to be circled, nor campfires doused early, nor babies' cries muffled against the feared Indian attacks. Nor did they have to go through the familiar morning routine of an early breakfast, rounding up and harnessing the oxen in order to get an advantageous position in the line of wagons, so that they would not have to travel in the dust raised by those in front of them. One woman wrote of the peace and beauty of viewing the twinkling lights of hundreds of campfires spread out before her as she sat resting on a bluff above the river.

From Wascopam Mission, the emigrants had three choices: to take the rough and tricky waters of the Columbia downstream, or to take one of the two hazardous foot trails across the Cascades: one to the north of Mt. Hood, which passed through the Hood River Valley and Lolo Pass (used earlier by Daniel Lee to bring cattle up from Oregon City), or the track around the south flank of the mountain. The first foot trail was the more direct, but the more hazardous, going over rugged mountain ridges and steep canyons. The easier southern route had more grass available for cattle, but had swampy areas where the cattle could bog down. If the emigrants were late in arriving at The Dalles, either of the land routes could be covered in snow. And neither of the routes were wagon trails – at least at first.

The route along the river followed Indian trails, which did not always lead where emigrants desired to go. One diary tells of driving cattle along the south side of the Columbia River, following such trails. However, it was not always clear which of the branching trails to take, and the cattle herd ended up in a huckleberry patch high on the mountainside. It had to retrace its steps, thus losing a day's travel.

When Samuel Barlow, Joel Palmer and others arrived at The Dalles in the fall of 1845, they found at least 60 families waiting to be ferried downstream. Advised by the mission that it was possible to go around the south side of Mt. Hood, three different groups started south, but soon joined up with each other in the vicinity of Tygh Creek, making a party of some 30 wagons. Some turned back, but Samuel Barlow and Joel Palmer kept on, eventually reaching Oregon City on foot and horseback and obtaining relief supplies for the people who had been left back with the wagons at Fort Deposit, just east of the summit of Mt. Hood.

The following spring work on clearing the road continued, making it possible

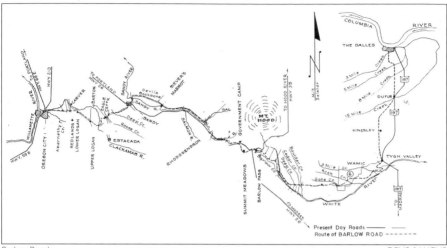

Barlow Road   CCHS & WCHS

for wagons to cross, even though at Laurel Hill, the descent was so steep that wagons had to be roped to trees to slow their progress downhill. In 1846 a tollgate was also built (rather ironic, since Barlow had apparently objected to the fees charged by the ferrymen for passage downstream). Charges were $5 a wagon, and 10 cents per head of livestock.[7]

Once the Barlow Road over the south flank of Mt. Hood was established, emigrants could by-pass The Dalles altogether by crossing the Deschutes in the area of Sherar's Bridge and pick up the Barlow Road near Tygh Valley. Some, but not the majority, chose to take this short cut, and were at first ferried across the river by Indians with canoes. Later a bridge was built.[8]

The river route, the most hazardous of them all, was also the one most often chosen. In the first years, emigrants could hire an Indian canoe or one

Sherars Bridge on the Deschutes River, 1890.   WCPA

of the few bateaux which the mission had at its disposal, or construct a crude raft of driftwood logs lashed together, on which they would load their wagons, families and belongings, often sharing the raft with several other families. They would drift downstream to the Cascades (presently Cascade Locks) where they would have to reassemble their wagons and portage around the rough waters. If they had arrived at The Dalles late in the season, rain and wind would delay the trip downstream, and emigrants were forced to walk in deep mud around the Cascades. Cattle would be driven along the south bank of the river, around Shell Rock Mountain, but at that point would often have to swim across the Columbia. The cattle would then walk along Indian trails on the north side of the river to a point across from the mouth of the Sandy River or further on to Fort Vancouver, and then would swim or be ferried back across to Oregon.

The 1847-1850 journal of Elizabeth Dixson Smith Greer illustrates the hardships of the journey down the Columbia:

"*October 24. We cross falls of Shutes River [Deschutes]. It was high, rapid and dangerous. The water came near to the tops of the wagon beds...*

October 27. Passed The Dalles Mission where two white families lived with the Indians. It looks like starvation.

October 28. Here are a great many immigrants camped, some making rafts, others going down in boats which have been sent up by speculators.

October 29. Rained most all day. Cold weather.

October 30. Rainy day. Men making rafts. Women cooking and washing and babies crying. Indians bartering potatoes for shirts. They must have a good shirt for a pack of potatoes.

October 31. Snow close by on the mountains. We should have gone over the mountains with our wagons, but they are covered with snow and we must go down by water and drive our cattle over the mountains.

November 1. We are lying by waiting for the wind to blow down stream in order that we may embark with our raft.

November 2. We took off our wagon wheels, laid them on the raft, placed the wagon beds on them and started. There are three families of us Adam Polk, Russell Welch, and ourselves, on twelve logs eighteen inches through and forty feet long. The water runs three inches over our raft.

November 3. Still lying by waiting for calm. Cold and disagreeable weather.

November 4. Rain all day. Laid by...

November 5. Still lying by waiting for calm weather. Mr. Polk very sick.

November 7. Put out in tough weather. Moved a few miles. The water so rough that we were forced to land. No one to man the raft but my husband and my oldest boy, sixteen years old. Russell Welch and our youngest boys are driving our cattle over the mountains...

November 8. We are still lying at anchor, waiting for the wind to fall...

November 9. *Finds us still in trouble. Waves dashing over our raft and we already stinting ourselves in provisions….Tonight about dusk Adam Polk expired….*

November 10. *Finds us still waiting for calm weather… [Later] the water had become calm and we started once more, but the wind soon began to blow and we were forced to land. My husband and boy were an hour and a half after dark getting the raft landed and made fast while the water ran knee-deep over our raft, the wind blew and it was freezing cold. We women and children did not attempt to get out of the wagons tonight.*

November 11. *Laid by most all day. Started this evening. Ran about three miles and landed after dark. Here we found Welch and our cattle, for they could not be driving farther on this side of the mountain. Here was a ferry for the purpose of ferrying immigrant's cattle.*

November 12. *Ferried our cattle across the Columbia and buried Mr. Polk. Rained all day….*

November 13. *We got the ferryman to shift our load onto their boat and take us down to the falls….Rain all day.*

November 18. *My husband is sick. It rains and snows. We start around the falls this morning with our wagons. We have five miles to go. I carry my babe and lead, or rather carry another through snow, mud and water almost to my knees. It is the worst road a team could possibly travel. I went ahead with my children and I was afraid to look behind me for fear of seeing the wagons overturn into the mud and water with everything in them. My children gave out with cold and fatigue and could not travel, and the boys had to unhitch the oxen and bring them and carry the children on to camp. I was so cold and numb that I would not tell by feeling them that I had any feet. We started this morning at sunrise and did not camp until after dark, and there was not one dry thread on one of us - not even on the babe. I had carried my babe and I was so fatigued that I could scarcely speak or step. When I got here, I found my husband lying in Welch's wagon very sick…I have not told half we suffered. I am not adequate to the task….*

November 19. *My husband is sick and can have but little care. Rain all day.*

November 20. *Rain all day…. I froze or chilled my feet so that I cannot wear a shoe, so have to go around in the cold water in my bare feet.*

[Elizabeth made it to the Willamette Valley, but her husband never recovered.]

February 1. *Rain all day. This day, my dear husband, my last remaining friend, died.*

February 2. *Today we buried my earthly companion…."* [9]

Sometimes a handful of people elected to winter over in The Dalles. Often they would watch over cattle left by their friends or relatives, who would then return to get them after the winter snows or heavy rains no longer posed such a great threat. These few families would construct crude shelters to live in, often in a sheltered area along Mill Creek - or a lucky few would be housed at the mission, or in later years, at Fort Dalles. However, in the early years none of these emigrants chose to settle - the first permanent resident is not recorded until 1847.

Elizabeth Laughlin Lord recalls wintering over at The Dalles in the year 1850:

"…The soldiers were quartered in tents while waiting for a mill to be built so they could secure sawed lumber. Over 100 emigrants and others were employed that winter to build the mill, to erect quarters for the men, a barn for the horses, a mess house and a cottage for the commanding officer…[10] *While hunting ducks and geese, father noticed Crate's Point and thought it was about five miles from the post. He decided to stay there for the winter, so we moved camp down there. He began cutting trees and shaping logs for a house…This work was interrupted, as he had to hunt for game to supply the table and made an occasional trip to Olney's store for supplies."*[11]

"Later that fall the Laughlins learned that they were on the military reservation property, and moved temporarily to a log house across from the fort, not far from where the Pioneer Cemetery is now. Soon Mrs. Laughlin was hired to cook for the soldiers, and the family was then housed at the fort for the winter."[12]

Early Logging   JW

Year after year, emigrants came westward over the Oregon Trail, doubling and redoubling the population of Oregon. In later years, some of the emigrants settled in Eastern Oregon, bringing the Columbia Plateau under cultivation, or settled in The Dalles. Although the majority of the emigrants came by wagon trail in the 1840s, 50s and 60s, the wagons continued to come even after the railroad was completed across the west. But the journey for these later emigrants was much changed from that of the early pioneers. By the late 1800s settlements had sprung up along the way where supplies could be purchased and mules and horses often replaced the oxen of the early emigrants. The fear of Indian attack was greatly diminished and finally non-existent, and when they arrived at the Columbia River, they could load their wagons and animals on one of the many steamboats going downstream.

George Cooper's crew loading watermelons, 1891.   WCPA

1   James Nesmith, in a speech to the Oregon Pioneer Association in 1875, "History of the Great Migration of 1843", www.oregon.gov/ODOT/CS/SSB/Oregon_Trail.shtml. 13 August 2011.

2   Lavender, p. 343.

3   Wm. Lyman, p. 148.

4   Donna Wojcik Montgomery, *Brazen Overlanders*, (Maryland: Heritage Books, 1992), p.319. A quote from the *St. Joseph Missouri Gazette,* August 21, 1846.

5   John C. Fremont, and John Torrey, and James Hall, *Report of the Exploring Expedition to the Rocky Mountains.* (Blair & Rives, 1845) Document 166. p. 194.

6   Montgomery, p. 308.

7   Johansen, p. 156.

8   John Fitzgerald Due, *Roads and Rails South from Columbia,* (Bend, OR: Maverick Publications, 1991), p. 46.

9   Theodore Thurston Greer, *Fifty Years in Oregon; Experiences, Observations and Commentaries.* (NY: Neale Publishing, 1912), p. 41.

10   Elizabeth Laughlin-Lord, *Reminiscences of Eastern Oregon,* (Portland, OR: Irwin-Hodson, 1903), p. 80.

11   Ibid., p. 72.

12   Ibid., p. 83.

9

FORT DALLES

The Indians were rarely concerned about the fur trappers, explorers or missionaries that they encountered, but when the great numbers of settlers began to arrive, the Natives' attitude gradually turned to hostility. Permanent settlers were a threat to their way of life, and they soon learned that the Western concept of land ownership was in total conflict with their understanding of land stewardship.

Early wagon train   WCPA

According to Frances Fuller Victor, "*the root of the troubles between missionaries and the natives was not at any time in their religious differences, which was really a side issue…, which alone need never have endangered the peace on the country. The real cause of ill feeling between the Indians and their Protestant teachers was the continued misunderstanding concerning the ownership of land and the accumulation of property… No one had appeared to purchase the lands occupied by the missions, nor had any ships arrived laden with Indian goods and farming implements for their benefit.*"[1]

The relatively large number of emigrants who arrived in 1842 disturbed the Cayuses around the Whitman mission enough that they burned the mission flour mill and destroyed much of the grain. Narcissa Whitman took refuge with the Methodist missionaries at The Dalles during the winter of 1842-43, while her husband went East to plead for the future of the mission.

The position of the white settlers was expressed by New York Morning News editor, John L. Sullivan in 1845: "*It is our manifest destiny to overspread and possess the whole of the continent which Providence has given us for the great experiment of liberty.*"

The impending conflict between the whites and the Native Americans came to a crisis point with the Whitman massacre in November, 1847. When news of the tragedy spread, a volunteer militia company was formed immediately, authorized by the Provisional Territorial Legislature, and sent to The Dalles, under the command of Major H.A.G. Lee. In order to protect the emigrants and their property, the legislature called for a regiment. Fortunately, a peace-keeping mission led by Joel Palmer, was also appointed and assigned to precede the military force. That group was being led by Colonel Cornelius Gilliam, into the Indian area, to reassure friendly Indians that the aim was to find those guilty for the attack. After a few skirmishes, the commissioners eventually succeeded in that aim, defusing the immediate situation.

When news of the massacre reached the east, it shocked the nation, and prodded the National Congress into passing the Organic Act of 1848, which established the Oregon Territory. With the Oregon Territory recognized as a part of the United States, the federal government now had the responsibility to guarantee military protection to its citizens, and so organized a series of military posts in the new territory. Fort Dalles was one of these posts established in 1850 under the command of Major S.S. Tucker as Camp Drum, named in honor of Captain Simon H. Drum, who had been killed on an assault on Mexico City in 1847.

Old Fort Dalles, 1849-1868   WCPA

It was manned during the first year by two companies of Mounted Rifles. Its main function during this first year was to give timely assistance to the many emigrants who, "*had consumed their last biscuit, and had not as much as a bacon rine (sic) to grease their wagons....*"[2] The decaying mission buildings would shelter only a few people, so the military companies, as well as emigrants wintering over, helped build the crude quarters which were to provide shelter for the soldiers for a number of years. In the spring the Mounted Rifles were dispatched elsewhere, and the post was left to a small artillery detachment of a dozen or so men. Lt. J.J. Woods, their commander, listed the following buildings in 1851:

"One 124'x20' log structure with unfinished floors and ceilings, used as officer's quarters.

A 140'x20' frame house with unfinished ceiling, used as quarters for the men.

A 36'x18' frame house, without ceiling.

A shingled slab storehouse, 36'x 18'.

A 30'x107' frame stable with loft and unfinished stalls.

Two sheds used as blacksmith's and carpenters' shops.

A sawmill.

An unfinished frame store house, 120'x24'."[3]

The fort was apparently in much the same situation in 1855, increased only by one more barracks and a hospital, when Captain Jordan, who had arrived with Colonel George Wright, was stationed here with 275 men and 11 officers. Of the officer's quarters he wrote: *"The Officers (now including myself) twelve in number, four of whom were Captains, were quartered in one building, a shabby log hovel divided into 6 rooms, each 18' x 19'6" and one room 17' x 13' with a small shed room attached in a frame extension. Two of the larger rooms being occupied by one of the Captains with his family, there remained but five rooms for the occupation of eleven Officers, entitled to fourteen; consequently, these Officers were huddled together as many as three in a room…and that room the worst that I have ever seen occupied as quarters in the army; unspeakably mean and uncomfortable, and grossly devoid of that privacy which civilized people require, not only in the connexion of its communism of occupancy, but with respect to occupancy of adjoining rooms! In one of these rooms I was forced to live last winter with my family, to the serious detriment of my health, as it could not be made comfortably warm."*[4] The troops lived in similar crowded and uncomfortable conditions.

The federal directive that established Camp Drum specified that military reservations be ten miles square. In the case of The Dalles, this took a territory that was an area greater than the current city limits, and included all the landing spots on the river. Complaints over the size of the reserve were voiced, and finally in 1853, Congress provided that military reserves be reduced to 20 acres, except for forts, which could be 640 acres. Although the commander at the time,

Guard House. The iron grill is located at Ft. Dalles Museum.　　　WCPA

43

Major Alvord, felt that this law did not properly apply east of the Cascade Mountains, he did take the precaution of changing the designation from camp to fort.[5]

By 1855, increased Indian hostility in the newly established Washington territory brought Fort Dalles into a primary position of key defense of the interior. Colonel George Wright was directed to bring and keep peace in the interior, with the orders that, *"you will establish the Head Quarters of your Regiment at The Dalles, where all the troops intended for the Indian Country will be concentrated."*[6]

Colonel Wright moved his troops north, leaving Captain Thomas Jordan, the assistant quartermaster and the only officer left at the fort, in charge. It was under Captain Jordan that plans were drawn up to transform Fort Dalles from, *"the most unattractive on the Pacific"* to one which would have officers'

Col. George Wright   DM

quarters, *"in cottage form.... arranged in every way to promote the convenience for those for whom they are intended...and for taste superior to those we have seen at any other post."*[7] Together with immigrant Louis Scholl, Jordan made plans to reproduce the picturesque cottage style then popular in the East. Scholl adapted the style of the cottage residences to barracks, guardhouse, storehouse, and even stables.

So impressive a building program was certain to bring repercussions. Jordan was warned about the costs of the project: *"Economy must be studied, and as that District has already cost a large amount, it is to be hoped that every effort will be made to curtail expenses."*[8]

Large amounts of money were funneled into the post. For over seven months, Jordan had an average payroll of over $14,000 a month for civilian workers alone. When told to discharge all civilians not "indispensable", Colonel Wright replied: *"It must be borne in mind that [because of the distances] Captain Jordan has some 700 public animals to look after. Thus it will be perceived, that the number of teamsters, packers, herders, and other persons employed in connection with supplying the advanced posts, although reported here, do not justify the statement that the "expenses of the Post are enormous". After deducting from the number of employees reported, all those constantly on the road, still we must recollect that to keep in repair all our means of transportation, it requires the constant service of*

Col. Wrights home at Ft. Dalles   DM

carpenters, wheel wrights, saddlers, blacksmiths &c; besides, we have to build large
boats, which accompany the wagon trains; ... Captain Jordan and his clerks have
labored with an intensity of application, rarely closing the office before 10 or 12
o'clock at night – "office hours" are unknown, even Sundays have not been days of
rest."[9]

Undoubtedly, the construction activity and the size of the fort brought a
great deal of money into The Dalles during the late 1850s. The fort's civilian
employees earned a monthly payroll from March 1856 to December 1858 which
totaled about $340,000. Further sums went to local transportation contracts,
as well as the actual payment to the troops themselves. Oregon newspapers
carried want ads for carpenters and joiners at the wage of $4 - $6 a day.

The threat of Indian hostility had brought importance to Fort Dalles;
although the Indians in the immediate vicinity were not hostile. The Yakima
Indian wars continued throughout the decade, and Fort Dalles continued to
be the center through which men, animals, supplies, and equipment would
arrive and be distributed to posts inland, such as Fort Simcoe and Walla Walla.
However, in the spring of 1859, an order from the Secretary of War stated that,
"all expenditures on account of the erection of quarters and barracks at Fort Dalles,
Oregon, be suspended until further orders."[10] But Fort Dalles did not disappear
immediately. The discovery of gold in Idaho and Eastern Oregon meant that the
military was still necessary for protection of Americans. The fort became inactive
in the summer of 1867, with only a caretaker remaining. Three larger officers'
quarters had burned by the end of that year. Eventually, its lands were sold or
deeded to the Catholic mission and the City of The Dalles, and other buildings
were simply absorbed by the city and its settlers and used for building materials.

Only the old Surgeon's Quarters remain, located at West 15th and Garrison Streets. It was described as, *"one of the loveliest little buildings in state."*[11] The original part of the Moody House (also known as the Rorick House) at 300 West 13th Street was built by a non-commissioned officer at Camp Drum in 1850. That section of the house is the oldest structure in The Dalles, and was given to the Wasco County Historical Society. It is open to the public for special occasions, opening its doors for the first time in the spring of 1993.

Old Fort Dalles Surgeon's Quarters, now a museum at W. 15th & Garrison Streets, The Dalles, OR.　　WJ

Rorick House. The oldest structure in The Dalles, 1850. Presently a museum at 300 W. 13th St.　　CW

"Built by lt U.S. Grant and Geo. Snipes 1854"   CW

One bit of local trivia: Ulysses S. Grant spent two weeks at Fort Dalles while on a tour of inspection. A stone in a small block building, commemorating this visit, can be found west of The Dalles in Rowena.

1   Frances Fuller-Victor, *The Early Indian Wars of Oregon. Compiled from the Oregon Archives and Other Original Sources: With Muster Rolls* (Salem, OR: F.C. Baker, 1894), p. 29.

2   Pricilla Knuth, *Picturesque Frontier: The Army's Fort Dalles,* (Portland, OR: Oregon Historical Society Press, 1987) p. 7.

3   Ibid., p. 10.

4   Ibid., p. 45.

5   Ibid., p. 10.

6   Ibid., p. 26.

7   Ibid., p. 30.

8   Ibid., p. 42.

9   Ibid., p. 42-43.

10   Ibid., p. 67.

11   Ibid., p. 69.

SETTLERS

1898. Prospector leaving Antelope, OR, en route to the gold mines.   LCD

With all the traffic of the Oregon Trail migration; the military, traders and explorers, it seems strange that there were few permanent settlers before 1850.

The first record of a permanent settler in The Dalles area is of a French trapper, Joseph Lavendure. He established a land claim, built a log cabin and fenced some land in 1846. But the lure of gold discoveries in California tempted him away, and he was apparently never heard from again.

The second settler was Nathan Olney, who, at age 20, had come with the Great Migration of 1843. Although, according to a biography by Roscoe Sheller, Olney is not listed in Nesmith's roll call of "Adult Male Immigrants of 1843. He came again with the wagon train in 1845, although that year he chose to accompany the ill-fated Stephen Meek party. In 1847 he took up a land claim on what was subsequently known as the John Irvine place". [1] After that date, emigrants mention stopping at Olney's store for supplies. He also went to the gold fields in California, but returned to retain his claim. Later he joined the military effort in the Indian Wars. After the establishment of Wasco County, he held a number of elected offices. His career as ferry owner was on the Deschutes. He and his brother Cyrus received authority from the legislature in January, 1852 "to establish and keep a ferry across the River Deschutes at such a point as they shall select within five miles of the falls to open a more direct route to the Cascade Mountains". The Olneys did not have to keep the ferry running at all times, but had to have it ready during emigrating season. They placed the ferry at the mouth of the Deschutes just below the swift water. They also had a ferry of sorts near the present Sherar's bridge area, probably below the falls and near the mouth of Buck Hollow, where the trail came to the river. At first the rate was $5.00 per wagon, but in December 1852 was lowered to $1.50 because of the many immigrants, or perhaps because of the shortage of them by December. Whatever the reason for the reduction in rate, the ferry business was lucrative. Nathan Olney sold his ferry to William Nix, also known as Bill Nixon, in 1854. In 1856, Victor Trevitt, Orland Humason and John Sims acquired the right to build a bridge across the Deschutes near Emigrant Crossing, within five miles of the mouth of the river.[2] In 1858-59, Nix built a bridge near the mouth of the Deschutes, where the Miller Bridge later stood.

That Olney must have been a colorful character can be seen in the following recollection of Elizabeth Laughlin Lord: *"I have frequently mentioned Nathan Olney, who came to The Dalles in 1847. He was a prominent man in the country at that time, handsome, intelligent, genial, and a general favorite with men; but owing to his domestic relations he was not usually sought by women. However, I recollect one exception, which I will give. At the hotel Thompkins… there was a lady of uncertain age, supposed to be a maiden, who had either come for her health or fortune hunting. She was romantic and susceptible; she thought she was in love with Captain Olney, and showed her preference in many ways on every occasion. Olney thought it very amusing for a time to flirt with her, but when everyone laughed about it, he grew tired of the play and I expect, feared trouble, for the laws at that time were construed in such a way that if a woman could prove that a single man had given her the name of wife, even in a joke, she was legally such. Olney was not married to his Indian wife then, and Indians had no legal rights at that time. Whether he planned his line of conduct or whether accident led up to part of it, I cannot say.*

One day he rode into town, accompanied by his squaw and her babe. He took them to the hotel, ushered them into the ladies' parlor, got her a chair, and with a waive [sic] of his hand and extremely polite bow said, "Ladies, Mrs. Olney". After emptying his pockets of a quantity of silver and gold into her lap he took leave. The woman tied the money loosely into a large handkerchief and threw it on the floor for the baby to play with. After a time she went out and shopped for an hour or two.

At supper time Mr. Olney came back apparently very intoxicated, and professed to be afraid to go into the house; he finally perched himself on top of a pile of cordwood in front, ordered his supper brought out to him, and ate it, talking and joking with the crowd gathered to enjoy the fun. After he had finished, his wife came out and said, "Come, Mr. Olney, we go home now." And he got down off the wood and walked away with her. The gentle maiden took the boat the following morning, and The Dalles knew her no more.

A few years later, Mr. Olney came to the conclusion that he was fitted to live a better life than he was then living. Times were changing. The country was settling up, and he craved the society of white women as well as white men. So he sent Annette to the reservation. They had two children at this time. He kept the elder and let her keep the babe. This man had left home at fifteen years of age and grown up on the frontier, respected and well treated by men, never realizing the light in which he stood with refined women.

After he had, as it were, swept and garnished his home, he set about finding a wife. After several refusals he discovered a lady who accepted him and after one week they were married, on the first day of April, 1856. They were separated within less than a month. A divorce followed, and the Indian woman returned to a place in his home. After spending the following winter in the Sandwich Islands (a law having in the meantime been enacted by Congress that men should not be allowed to live with Indian women without being married to them), in the spring Nathan Olney and his two younger brothers took their squaws down to a justice of the peace and were married."[3]

Nathan Olney had a varied career of storekeeper, ferry owner, sheriff, Indian agent, fur trader, explorer, farmer, and cattle rancher. But it was as an Indian trader that he was best known. After the Whitman massacre, he led a group of volunteers to help protect an emigrant train, and was hit in the head by an arrow, which could not be removed since it was too close to the brain. His older

Ben Snipes home at 218 W. 4th St., presently Anzac Tea Parlor.   PK

brother Cyrus, a lawyer and territorial judge, tried to get a fur trading venture started so that Nathan could stop working so strenuously. Since Nathan had an Indian wife, getting the furs was no problem. They took a shipment of furs to Hawaii (probably meant for the Chinese market) and sold them, returning to Oregon some time later. However, Nathan's health did not improve, and the trading business ended. Nathan Olney died in 1866 after a riding accident while rounding up his cattle. The fall caused the arrow to penetrate his brain.[4]

Ben Snipes arrived in Oregon in 1852 as a 17 year old boy determined to make his fortune. By the time he found his brother George in the Dalles City in January of 1855, he was purchasing cattle and claimed the grassland of the Simcoe Hills and the Yakima Valley to run his herd. He acquired thousands of head of cattle and horses and made and lost several fortunes supplying meat to the gold miners in British Columbia and Montana. Prices fluctuated greatly with the severe winters of 1861, 1871 and 1894, when thousands of cattle and horses died because of freezing temperatures and deep snow. He and his wife, Mary Parrot Snipes are buried at the Odd Fellows Cemetery in The Dalles.[5]

George Snipes, 1865 · WCPA

George Snipes did not intend to come to Oregon as his brother Ben Snipes did in 1852. George's future wife's father took his family to Oregon to get her away from the man he did not want her to marry. George was determined to find her and signed on to the next wagon train leaving Council Bluffs. At the Deschutes River he met Nathan Olney, a friend from his past, who helped George find Martha Imbler and helped her escape her father's wagon train. George and Martha were married before morning by the minister with George's wagon train. She had outsmarted her father, who was very upset when he discovered what had happened. They settled at Rowena and raised 13 children.[6]

In 1850, Mr. J.W. Coventon described the scene at The Dalles where he camped for a short time by the mouth of Mill Creek, near the point where emigrants abandoned their horses and wagons and proceeded by way of the river to the Willamette Valley. Coventon wrote that, *"there were about one*

Martha Imbler Snipes · WCPA

hundred old wagons in every stage of dilapidation

George Snipes Prune Orchard, Chenoweth Road, 1910.   WCPA

scattered about the place where now stands The Dalles. Crippled and half starved cows and oxen were seen on the hillsides. There was one cabin on Mill Creek, with a few articles of merchandise for sale." Since the only residence at the time in The Dalles was Nathan Olney's, this cabin was undoubtedly his store.[7] At the time the Laughlin family arrived in 1850, the store was on Olney Creek, now called Chenoweth Creek.

During the same year William Laughlin started to build a cabin at Crate's Point, but was informed that this land was part of the military reservation, and abandoned the building. Crate's Point was named for Edward Crate, who had been employed by the Hudson's Bay Company at one time. He and his wife, Elizabeth, arrived at The Dalles in 1849, and in 1850 received the first wife-husband Donation Land Claim in the area; 320 acres for him and 320 acres for her. They raised 14 children, and Mr. Crate worked ferrying emigrants, soldiers, and supplies between The Dalles and Fort Vancouver.

Edward Crate   WCPA

The Donation Land Claim Law granted 320 acres of land to any male over 18 years old who had settled on a piece of land in Oregon Territory before 1855, on the condition he would cultivate it and live on it for four years. If he was married, his wife also received 320 acres -- in her own name! -- a remarkably progressive law for that time. One immigrant rued that her husband had chosen to become a store-keeper rather than a farmer -- now she was dependent on him forever.

In 1851-52, Justin Chenoweth was a U.S. mail carrier who lived "in a sort of cave on the banks of the river, below a residence site later occupied by Mr. Klindt, at the mouth of a creek which now bears his name"... Chenoweth Creek. By the fall of 1852 Chenoweth had built a large home there, and for some time tried to create a town in that area. Failing in his efforts he moved away. [8]

Elizabeth Lord remembers Justin Chenoweth: *"In 1851 we had a mail route established. The carrier had a boat which he sailed when there was wind, and when there was none he rowed. Remembering him as I do, I think he must have whistled up a breeze most of the time, even if he had to force it with a dollar to an Indian to row for him. The mail carrier was Justin Chenoweth.*[9]

In 1854, Charles W. Denton set out his first fruit orchard on Mill Creek. In the previous year D. Bolton was said to have raised the first commercial crop of wheat east of the cascades and established an extensive farm on Fifteen Mile Creek. The missionaries had raised wheat for their own use at the Methodist mission. In 1852, George Snipes settled on his place, seven miles below The Dalles. With these firsts, and the coming of steamboat transportation, the town of The Dalles began to grow quite rapidly.

Walter and son, Henry Klindt on their farm west of The Dalles.   PK

Fishing nets draped for drying at Klindt's fishing dock on the Columbia River.　　　　PK

Hayfield on Klindt's farm near the mouth of Chenoweth Creek　　　　PK

Henry Klindt arrived in Dalles City via wagon train in 1862, after first traveling to the California gold mines in 1859, and then returning to Iowa. A tornado had destroyed his property in Iowa, so he and his wife Doris Stottenberg, set out for Oregon. They were both natives of Germany. Henry was a truck gardener and stone mason and he settled on the Columbia River west of The Dalles on what is now the Port of The Dalles property. He is credited for having built the Getchell Building which still stands at First and Washington Streets, north of the railroad tracks. Henry owned approximately one mile of riverfront, which reached to Taylor Lakes west of The Dalles.

Klindt family home and cistern, now Port of The Dalles offices on Klindt Drive.

WJ

Henry's son, Walter Klindt, later became a commercial fisherman and rented the farm out to a Japanese farmer. In 1955 it became illegal for non-Natives to fish above the Bonneville Dam, ending Walter Klindt's fishing business.

Walter's son, Henry Klindt, the third generation, worked at the bank until the Depression and then he took the farm back and converted it to raising two crops of onions each year. In 1962, the family was forced to sell 365 acres, 100 of it tillable, to the Port of The Dalles, under threat of condemnation. The stone house was built in 1939 for Henry and Phyllis Klindt and since the Port did not develop the property until the late 1980s, after the bond issue was approved, the family made arrangements to stay in the house until that time. This house became the Port office headquarters. The house, the packing shed and the octagonal cistern still remain on this site.

1   Shaver, p. 106.

2   Giles French, *The Golden Land: A History of Sherman County, Oregon*, (Portland, OR: Oregon Historical Society, 1958) pp. 24-25.

3   Shaver, p. 106.

4   Sidney Teiser, "Cyrus Olney, Associate Justice of Oregon Territory Supreme Court", *Oregon Historical Quarterly* (Portland, OR: Abbot, Kerns & Bell, 1963), Vol. 64, pp. 311-318.

5   Rosco Shiller, *Ben Snipes Northwest Cattle King*, (Portland, OR: Binford & Mort, 1957), p. 145.

6   Ibid., p. 18-22.

7   Wm. H. McNeal, "Some Historical Notes Wasco County", *Oregon Historical Quarterly* (Portland, OR: Abbot, Kerns & Bell, 1955), Vol. 56, pp. 81-85. McNeal places Olney's house and store on the banks of Mill Creek, near First Street; unfortunately, much of McNeal's information is not reliable and generally undocumented.

8   Shaver, p. 107.

9   Ibid., p. 129.

11

WASCO, THE MOTHER OF COUNTIES

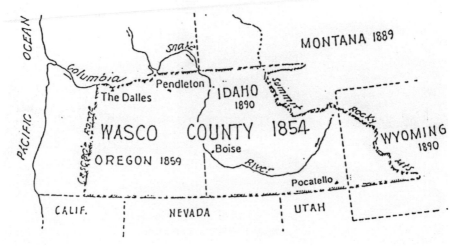

Original Wasco County   JW

Wasco County was established by the Oregon Territorial Legislature in 1854, and at that time was the largest county in the United States, extending from the Cascade Range east to the crest of the Rocky Mountains, bounded by the 46th parallel on the north, and the 42nd parallel on the south; it included eastern Oregon, half of Idaho, and parts of Wyoming and Montana. The non-native population of the entire county at the time was probably less than 300, including many trappers in the employ of the Hudson's Bay Company. Less than 100 votes were cast in the first election for the County Board of Commissioners. The Dalles was named the county seat.

The first Board of Commissioners met in April of 1854, and had to address proceedings dealing with places as far away as Green River, Wyoming, and Salmon Falls, Idaho. It granted licenses to Orlando Humason to operate a ferry at Fort Boise, and established the fees to be charged; it granted a license to J. L. Henderson to keep a grocery at The Dalles; and it granted Justin Chenoweth a license to keep a ferry at The Dalles for a term of two years - with the following rates: *"For each loose animal one dollar; for horses with rider one dollar and fifty cents; horse with pack, sheep or hog, twenty-five cents, for a man fifty cents"*.[1]

Stuck in the mud. 1880's   WCPA

July 4th Parade, 1877   DM

A few years later the commissioners were forced to assess property taxes in order to build a county courthouse with an adequate jail. The first Wasco County Court House, a modest two-story frame structure, was built in 1859 for $2500. It contained three jail cells on the first floor, as well as some county offices. The courtroom on the second floor was accessible only by an outside stairway. This room was also used by the newly founded Congregational Church for its services, and apparently the prisoners downstairs could hear the

The original courthouse, now a museum, stands near Mill Creek at 410 West 2nd Place. WJ

sermons, for at times the congregation could hear shouts of "Amen" coming up from the floor below. Others tell of hymns being interrupted by the prisoners singing songs in their own unique style.

Other than Nathan Olney's small stock of supplies, the first merchants at The Dalles were the sutlers at the military garrison. In 1851, Allen McKindlay received permission from the post authorities to erect a frame building near the intersection of what is now First and Court Streets, and stocked it with goods. Another settler, William R. Gibson, moved his log store down to the Landing at the foot of Union Street, and was subsequently bought out by Victor Trevitt. Also in 1852, W. D. Bigelow came with a small stock of goods, groceries, and liquors, and squatted, pitching a canvas house. He conducted a lucrative trade, and the next year built a conventional store with lumber.

A primitive hotel was built by John Tompkins in 1852. A traveler at the time described The Dalles as a dirty hamlet of a few miserable huts.

The pace of building was not exactly feverish at first. In 1853, a blacksmith's shop was added, a two-story frame house was begun - to be finished the following year and opened as The Dalles Hotel. In the fall of 1853, The Dalles was a city of tents, with signs describing their use: restaurants were the majority, but there were also stores and cattle buyers. In 1854, H.P. Isaacs opened a saloon and bowling alley in a two-story board house; this building later became the Western Hotel. During these years there was no platted town site: people built wherever they pleased. Citizens set about formulating plans for the division of property only in 1855.

Early Dalles City   JW

The discovery of gold near Fort Colville, in Washington Territory, 1854, attracted thousands to the area, and The Dalles became an important outfitting and shipping point. The discovery of gold in central Oregon and Idaho a few years later increased the traffic through the city, since the miners stocked up on supplies here before heading eastward.

Early Brewery Grade   JW

The Dalles was incorporated in 1857. By this time it had a population of about 250 people, with a number of businesses, centered on Main Street (First Street) and a block up on Union Street.

According to Elizabeth Laughlin Lord, "*for nearly a decade a decidedly low state of morality existed at The Dalles. The town was under domination of gamblers*

2nd Street, 1884   DM

2nd Street Parade   WCHM

and other representatives of the "tough" element. There were a number of murders and numerous cutting and shooting scrapes".[2]

In 1858, The Dalles had the following businesses: The Umatilla House, owned by A. J. Nixon; the Cushing Hotel and store; a restaurant and lodging house run by Colonel N.H. Gates; the Wasco Hotel, owned by A. H. Curtiss; the Bradford and Co. Steamboat office; the Bigelow grocery store; the Mount Hood Saloon, run by B. F. McCormick; the Powell and Co. saddle and harness shop; the Trevitt and Cowne saloon; the McAuliff grocery store; an assay office run by W.C. Moody; the P. Craig drug store; the H. P. Isaacs general merchandise store; the R.R. Thompson and Co. warehouse; a cigar store run by J. Juker (who was also the first immigrant to be naturalized in Wasco County); and the W. L. DeMoss bakery.[3]

French & Co. Bank, 1862-1922. 2nd & Washington   WCPA

Umatilla House lobby at 1st & Union.   WCPA

Kuck Saddle and Harness Shop.   WCPA

Wagon Wheel Shop   DM

Wagon Shop   DM

Gunning Blacksmith Shop, about 1908. 2nd & Laughlin   WCPA

1   Ibid., p. 111.

2   Ibid., p. 134.

3   Ibid., p. 134.

12

STEAMBOATS

Sternwheeler at Cascade Locks   DM

"Stewards lit fancy nickel lamps that hung from a rod down the middle of the saloon....Her decks were neatly railed, with cornices of gee-gawed scrollwork." [1]

Service was good and the ride magnificent from Portland to The Dalles, but passengers had to rise early to catch the boat at Portland. Freight loaded all night, and passengers began to arrive at 4:30; the boat left at 5:00 a.m.

"Usually passengers took breakfast from tables in the main saloon, and paid for the privilege, at first two bits, but later the price went up. Then, after the boat ran out of the Willamette into the Columbia and touched at the landing at Vancouver, they would begin to gather on deck, for already the spectacular scenery of gorge had become widely advertised. Slowly the fir-covered hills moved higher and closer to the river, and tall basalt outcrops and columns rose like flanking portals with many falls veiling down the face of the rocks. By then the sun was out, and the ladies strolled the deck while the gentlemen retreated to the bar. The O.S.N. (Oregon Steam Navigation Company) usually was engaged in a company battle about the bars; at first, Captain Ainsworth had been dead set against them, but after a few months the bars were installed and rented out, at a good stiff price, to concessionaires whose barkeepers also ranked the honorary title of "Captain".

At eleven o'clock the boat docked at Lower Cascades, where the train of the portage railway waited, and the passengers went ashore. There was no need to

hurry; all the fast freight had to be trundled by handcart out onto the wharf boat and into the stubby freight cars, and the job usually took an hour. If there was a great deal of freight, that which did not have a prepaid premium simply waited for another boat, usually a smaller one that worked only in the freight run. Then the small locomotive whistled and the train moved up the line, the passengers housed in elegant, light colored coaches.

At the Upper Cascade, everything had to be unloaded from the train and put into the second boat, and the passengers had another wait. Some spent it looking at

Multomah Falls, 1867.   DM

Sternwheeler at dock
DM

the churning rapids and the scenery; some took lunch at the hotel that stood by the landing. Some idly visited the blockhouse built after the attack of 1856. And some, no doubt, of the gentlemen went aboard the second boat to seek solace forward at another bar. Whatever they did, they had an hour or so to kill before the journey was resumed. By the time everything was ready, it was early afternoon, and it would be evening before the boat pulled up to the landing at The Dalles."[2]

From the 1860s on, travelers had lots of choices of places to stay overnight, but two were most popular. The grand Umatilla House, said to be the best outside of Portland, in spite of its notoriously friendly fleas and occasionally chummy bedbugs and lice. Another choice was the less showy and smaller Cosmopolitan Hotel, with 75 rooms, and such touches of luxury as a billiard

Bailey Gatzert passengers disembarking at Union St., The Dalles
JW

parlor and a ladies parlor, with piano. If a traveler was too late for either of these, there were others down the street.

The Umatilla House was first built in 1857, but remodeled and enlarged several times. When a traveler entered and would sign in, he saw the handsomest counter and most elegant key rack in the state. Single rooms were not available; a lucky traveler would have to share with only three strangers. The hotel had

123 rooms, a couple of baths, and the lavatory in the basement. The dining room was excellent, and during the gold rush days, they took in more money over their bar than all the rest of the hotels in The Dalles put together.

Situated at First and Union Streets, between the railroad tracks and the river, The Umatilla House burned in 1877,

Umatilla House Coach   JW

was rebuilt, but burned again in 1879. After arranging financing, a large crew of carpenters took only four months to rebuild an even larger structure than the one that burned. The new 141 room hotel was soon considered the best west of Minneapolis and north of San Francisco. The immense lobby had gilt-decorated walls and a fine array of furniture. The barroom was also profusely decorated,

Umatilla House Billiard Room   WCPA

and had an elaborate inlaid and carved pool table. This room served as a club and meeting place for locals as well as guests. The main dining room seated 250

people, and at times 16 waiters and 12 cooks were employed. The hotel was known for its excellent meals, in particular, its salmon dinners. Ice was brought from the ice caves near Mount Adams, and kept in sawdust in the basement. The ladies parlor was the main room on the second floor, reached by a wide winding stairway from the lobby.

Ornate legs and inlay on pool table.   WCPA

Its elegant furnishings were the pride of the hotel's owners. However, over the years, and especially after the decline of passenger traffic on the river, the business center of town grew east, away from the Umatilla House; the boat lines discontinued passenger service, and the old hotel grew too shabby to continue attracting guests. It finally closed to business, and in 1929 was ordered wrecked by its owner.[3]

However, in the 1860s and 1870s, the portage railway that went around the Narrows to Celilo met the steamboats in front of the Umatilla House. Thus passengers who were continuing on upstream could board the train at 5:00 a.m., and if no sand had been blown across the tracks, would reach Celilo in about an hour and a half, board the boat that would reach Umatilla by

Wool Wagons at Wasco Warehouse, 1890's   WCPA

afternoon, where, if he wished, a traveler could board the stage for Boise, Salt Lake City, or further east.

Meanwhile, The Dalles continued to grow. For the entire country east of the Cascade Range The Dalles was the center of trade. The thousands who passed through The Dalles on their way to the mines often returned to the City to spend the winter, bringing their gold dust with them. There were few coins, almost no paper money, and merchants took the dust itself in payment for goods.

Wool teams on old Brewery Grade, 1899   WCPA

In an interview with Fred Lockley, Col. Henry M. Dosch talked about this time: *"In the spring of 1864 I was working for Bloch, Miller & Company at The Dalles. At that time they had the largest store in Oregon. We not only handled general merchandise and miners' supplies, but we also operated the warehouse from which goods were taken by pack train to the mines. The Dalles had a permanent population at that time of about 2,500, but the streets were always thronged with transients on their way to and from the mines. There was more activity in The Dalles in a day than in Portland in a month. I had charge of buying the gold dust for the firm. This was a very responsible job, because it was not a mere matter of weighing out the gold dust -- it was a matter of deciding how much to pay for it so we could make a reasonable profit. Gold dust from Canyon City or Florence was worth $17 an ounce, while dust that looked equally good from other districts had an alloy of silver in it so that I only paid $10 an ounce for it. The reddish gold was also less valuable, as it had an alloy of copper...The saloons and merchants at The Dalles accepted gold dust in payment for their wares and we bought gold dust from them. At that time there was no currency in circulation whatever. There was of course gold coins from the one dollar gold piece to the fifty dollar gold slug, but most of the trading was done by the miners, fresh from the mines, with the dust that they themselves had washed or rocked out. The Dalles in those days was a wide open town. George Clayton ran the biggest gambling house in Eastern Oregon. You could get plenty of action on your gold dust in his place with poker, faro, three-card Monte, or you could bet your money on the small horses. The silver quarter was the smallest coin used. Cigars were 50 cents each, and drinks ranged from two bits to four bits each. Vic Trevitt ran the Mount Hood Saloon which was really a sort of gentlemen's club. He wouldn't allow a drunken man in the place, nor would he allow gambling..."* [4]

Prospecting miners from California, Mexico, the East Coast, and British Columbia came through The Dalles to try their luck in the mines. In the winter, many spent their time and gold dust in The Dalles, with the feeling of "easy come, easy go". Most of the miners were young, and felt that there was plenty more where that came from. All hotels and lodging houses were filled to capacity; it was not unusual to have as many as 10,000 people in town for short times.

Because of the amount of gold dust in the city, a movement to build a United States mint at The Dalles was started. As one writer put it, a somewhat cloudy-minded and spasmodic Congress appropriated $100,000 in 1865 to build the mint. Rock was brought from Mill Creek and a first story was built, at what is now 710 East Second Street, but then Congress had a change of heart. Deciding that the mint at San Francisco was enough; the site and the building

U.S. Mint Building, The Dalles   DM

were sold for a song. Later it was expanded and additional stories were built and the building was used as a flour mill and then storage for many years. In 2005, it was renovated to become a winery and tasting room.

By 1868, the gold fields in Idaho and Eastern Oregon began to play out, and The Dalles began to lose some of its glory as many drifted to the boom towns and mining camps in Montana. By 1870 the population had declined to 742, after an estimated high of 2,500 in 1866.

But the years of prosperity brought a number of civic improvements to the town. In 1862, the first water system was completed, bringing water to the city; the system became municipal in 1891. A franchise for a gas plant was issued in 1863, but was never completed, so the town relied on oil lamps until the electric light plant was completed in 1882. And curiously, in 1862, James S. Reynolds was granted a right of way to lay a plank sidewalk on Union Street from Second

Street to the low water mark on the Columbia, with the right to collect toll on this bit of sidewalk!

Even with the coming of the railroad in 1880, steamboats remained exceedingly popular until well into the twentieth century. Wheat had become a major crop and the railroads at first were not capable of transporting so much tonnage in a limited time. Large boats were built at The Dalles: the *Western Queen* in 1879, the *Hassalo* in 1880, the *Regulator* in 1891. For use on the Upper River, a number of steamboats were built at Celilo: the *Annie Faxon* and the *Spokane* in 1877, the *John Gates* and the *Harvest Queen* in 1878, the *Frederick K. Billings* in 1881, and the *Service,* the *Twin-Cities,* and the *Inland Empire* in 1908.

Wood Scow   WCHM

The opening of the Cascade Canal and Locks in 1896 was a great boon to river transport - now freight and passengers would not have to be transferred via portage railways from one boat to another at the Cascades. Cargo, which was loaded at The Dalles, could now reach the ocean with no further handling. Understandably, opening day called for great celebrations. Thousands assembled at Cascade Locks to watch the first steamers come through the locks. The Dalles brass band played and the Oregon National Guard fired salutes. The *Regulator,* from The Dalles was the first to enter the locks from above. The *Sara Dixon* made the first trip from Portland to The Dalles, accompanied by the *Regulator* and *Dalles City,* which had met it at Cascade Locks. At The Dalles, *"citizens had erected two handsome arches, brilliantly illuminated by electricity; through these marched one of the largest and most imposing parades ever before witnessed in the Inland Empire."* [5]

After the completion of the Cascade Canal and Locks, the only remaining obstruction to open river were the Narrows and Celilo Falls. The Dalles - Celilo

71

Parade on 2nd Street, The Dalles.

DM

Daily run from Portland to The Dalles and return. Fare was $1 each way including meals.

WCPA

First two boats through Celilo canal   DM

Canal, completed in 1915, was built to allow boats free passage to the upper Columbia.

In 1947, the sternwheeler Georgie Burton, the steamboat which had been launched in 1906, made her last trip up the Columbia River to The Dalles. It was a special ceremonial run, with a special crew and passengers taking part in this last journey.

"At Vancouver the Georgie Burton tied up at a wharf to take aboard a special crew of the old timers, men who loved the river and the steamers and were helping retire the boat in real style. Judge Fred Wilson was there; son of a steamboat captain, Judge Wilson inherited affection for steamers that passed beyond a hobby into a consuming purpose. Aboard the Burton, Judge Wilson knew his place and acted as purser. Men from the boats themselves took tricks at the wheel as the steamer went on up the river: Captain Winslow, Captain Fidler - seventeen years aboard the Burton as her commander - Captain McClintock, Captain Monical, all veterans on the river. And there were newspapermen aboard, of course, to cover the story and be in on the party. All along the river, people stood on the banks to watch her; school children turned out to see the steamer go by...On up the Columbia the Georgie Burton sloshed along while the fog thinned and the sky brightened. She passed familiar places, the sights passengers watched for and remembered, like Cape Horn and Multnomah Falls. She reached the lower Cascades and entered the tall lock of Bonneville Dam. Slowly the lock filled and the Georgie Burton slid out into the slack water beyond, riding over what had been the awesome Cascades, now nothing

more than a quiet pool. Off the starboard bow a line of masonry near the bank was all that remained above the water of the Cascade Locks…Beyond the point, to the port, the Upper Cascades and its reconstructed blockhouse, and a little farther the spot where the Indians came down to the river.…

Finally the Georgie Burton passed The Dalles, where the whole town turned out to watch, and went on to edge into a pool at the foot of Celilo Canal. There the voyage ended, the boat was at her last berth. Not quite the last, to be exact; shortly she would be drifted down to The Dalles, slid into a cradle, and towed up onto the land, to become a marine museum, a relic of the great days on the river, when The Dalles was a roaring river town and the big boats came and went. It was fitting that a steamboat should be preserved and that it should be at The Dalles. Diesel towboats might shove barges back and forth on the river, handling tonnage

The Umatilla navigating the Celilo Canal.   WCHM

greater than anything Ainsworth and the O.S. N. had even vaguely conceived, but the diesel towboat, compact and unemotionally utilitarian, somehow lacked the glamour and the glory of the white cabins, the tall stacks, and the flashing wheels of the steamboat. Still - who knows? - sometime a diesel towboat, her days of usefulness over, and her type disappearing, may be hauled up beside the Burton."[6]

---

1   Randall V. Mills, *Stern-Wheelers Up Columbia: A Century of Steamboating in the Oregon Country.* (Palo Alto, CA: Pacific Books, 1947), p. 48.

2   Ibid., pp. 43-44.

3   Martha Ferguson-McKeown, "The Historic Umatilla House at The Dalles", *Oregon Historical Quarterly.* (Salem, OR: Statesman Publishing Company, 1930), Vol. 31. pp. 37-41.

4   Fred Lockley, *History of the Columbia River Valley from The Dalles to the Sea.* (Chicago, IL: S.J. Clarke Publishing Co., 1928) pp. 930-931.

5   Shaver, p.123.

6   Mills, pp. 183-184.

FLOODS, FIRES AND FUTURE

Winter, 1911. East 2nd St., The Dalles   WCPA

"Mr. Ed Crate Sr., one of the French Canadian voyageurs, who came to this state with the Hudson's Bay Company, says in 1842 he landed bateaux at the foot of the bluff near the Methodist Church. This had been doubted until this year when, taking into consideration that there were no buildings here to furnish distinctive marks regarding particular localities, and that the contour of the bluff is much the same for a long distance, the feat was not only possible but probable." ...as reported in The Dalles Times-Mountaineer, June 10, 1894.[1]

According to the records kept by William Laughlin, the winter of 1861-62 was the most severe experienced by white settlers in the Northwest to that date. Laughlin's journals record sub-freezing temperatures for all of January and half of February, with the lowest temperature recorded at 30 below zero on January 17. Snow started falling in early December and continued throughout the winter, with snow recorded at 30 ½ inches deep on February 18. Nearly all the livestock died in the countryside, because they were not able to get food, and people suffered correspondingly. Because of the great amount of snow, the amount of water in the rivers rose dramatically in the early summer. The highest stage was 48 feet 10 inches above the low water mark, flooding Front and Second Streets, as well as part of Third Street.

Fire on 2nd Street, 1891   RN

In 1866, the river flooded again, and again in 1871, causing considerable damage. In 1871, half of the city was burned to the ground by fire. This first started in the Old Globe Hotel, at the corner of Second and Washington Streets, and destroyed all the east portion of town as far as Rev. Thomas Condon's residence on the corner of Third and Laughlin Streets. This edifice was saved only by the strenuous efforts of the citizens. The rows of handsome poplar trees surrounding the house were killed by the flames. Another flood in 1876 exceeded that of 1862, cresting at 51 feet 3 inches. After this instructive experience many businesses which had been located on Front Street now moved to Second Street, which became the main street of the city.

October 1878 saw another large fire, which originated in a saddler's shop and burned all the property between Federal and Washington Streets below Fourth Street. During this fire H. J. Waldron died from injuries caused by fighting the fire. Waldron's Drug Store was located in the old stone

Cosmopolitan Hotel Fire on 1st Street   WCPA

Waldron Drug Store, more recently known as the Getchell Bldg.
Located at 1st and Washington Streets.

CW

building which is still standing on the north side of the railroad tracks at the foot of Washington Street, having survived all the disastrous fires and floods to hit The Dalles.

May, 1879 saw yet another destructive fire - the most disastrous up to that point. Within three hours the business portion of The Dalles was laid waste - a mass of black and smoldering ruins. It broke out in the Pioneer Hotel, on Second Street, and the flames spread in all directions. However, since this was a boom period, businesses quickly rebuilt. The Oregon Railroad and Navigation Co. was extending lines both east and west of The Dalles, and the city was once again a supply depot for the workmen who were building the repair shops, round-houses, and numerous other buildings

O.R.&N. Train. The first train from Portland to New York, was in 1883.

JW

77

required for a rail center. Again, The Dalles gained the reputation of being a tough town, and robberies and homicides became a frequent occurrence. But during 1878-81, many new attractive business buildings were constructed.

The year 1880 saw double damage: a potentially serious fire, started by an arsonist, burned a number of buildings, but the fire department managed to control the fire. This fire in June was followed by a flood in July, which threatened to reach the same level as the one of 1876. It crested, however, at 48 feet, 7 ½ inches (lacking almost 3 feet of the 1876 level), but boats were still able to navigate Front Street.

More fires and floods of the early 1880s brought further damage to the downtown, but the years 1884-85 brought improvement. Many of the blocks which had burned in the preceding years were now rebuilt as brick or stone buildings, replacing the earlier wooden ones. Another

Umatilla House, 1894 Flood.   JW

The Dalles Times-Mountaineer   DM

fire in 1888 destroyed two blocks between Washington and Federal Streets, along Third Street, and crossing it, burned a number of residences and the Congregational Church.

But the building boom continued and in 1889 an elegant brick opera house was opened. When John Crate became a member of The Dalles police force in the mid-1880s, the town had thirty-two saloons.[2]

The Dalles Times-Mountaineer of January 1, 1889, summarized the prosperity of the town: *"The city now numbers over 4,000 population and boasts many modern improvements. Within the last few years solid brick blocks have been erected and places which were once grain fields embraced within the city limits. A good system of sidewalks has been constructed, streets have been graded, fire limits established and other strides made...two large brick warehouses have been erected for the storage of grain and wool. Every season of the year large quantities of the rich products of the surrounding country find their way to these buildings and create quite a stir in business life and send a large amount of money in circulation. Then the long established shops of the Oregon Railroad and Navigation Company give employment to several hundred men....The electric light system has been lately introduced and we have no doubt that when the arrangement is perfected it will add brilliancy to our stores and streets...Capital is not wanting. On a rough estimate there is $7,000,000 now the same as lying dormant, which might be invested in enterprises tending to increase the population and wealth. But the fatal lethargy appears to possess our businessmen...."[3]*

Another Fire   WCPA

Another destructive fire hit the city in January of 1890, destroying or damaging several buildings on the corner of Second and Washington. Finally, that year, the city decided, after years of deliberation, to organize a municipal water supply. According to a later article, the water system which was developed, *"has a sufficient amount of water to supply a city of 20,000 inhabitants, and besides the volume being large the quality is the best."[4]*

But this wonderful water system was not yet installed when the most destructive fire in the history of The Dalles, before or since, occurred on September 2, 1891. More than twenty blocks were burned to the ground, including many of the best business buildings. The fire started, apparently in a stable, on the east end of Second Street, and rapidly spread, fanned by the wind, southwest to Court Street, burning much of Second and Third Streets. The only buildings on Second Street which pre-date the fire of 1891 are those west of Federal. Many beautiful residences along Third Street were also burned.

The Dalles Times-Mountaineer, on the following day, September 3, 1891,

1891 Fire. Ruins of the Vogt Opera House.   WCPA

amid the detailed reports of the progress of the fire, the losses and the injuries, had an optimistic prediction: *"The prominence of The Dalles as a business point and commercial center depends on its natural situation, and floods cannot wash away or fires destroy this prestige. In two years we may expect to see a fairer city than ever raise out of the ashes of this terrible conflagration."*

But the newspaper was equally quick to lay blame: *"When fire has swallowed up property to the amount of $1,200,000, it is time to stop and moralize upon the cause. The department did all they possibly could to stop the progress of the conflagration; but the water supply was entirely inadequate... The fire department used Herculean efforts, but they were unavailing, for frequently the water would give out while the greatest acts to subdue the fury of the flames were being made.... A million dollars went up in flames, and if the Columbia river pumping system, adopted by the people a year ago, had been in operation not over $10,000 would*

Flood, 1894, West 2nd Street. St. Marys Academy & the old Catholic Church. WCPA

have been lost…Will our citizens profit by the lesson thus dearly taught by ruined business prospects and desolated hearthstones?"

Less than three years after the "big fire" came the "big flood" of 1894. The river had started rising in April, and was still rising at the end of May. Downtown merchants moved their goods to higher ground in anticipation of high water. Front Street was flooded completely; the only dry piece of Second Street was a small area near the Columbia Brewery. Third Street was completely inundated, except for a block between Court and Washington, and Fourth Street was covered to a large degree on the east and west ends. Due to the severe flooding we have little physical evidence of the Chinese workers who lived in the First Street area. The flood waters crested on June 6, at a height of 59 feet, 7 inches above low water mark. A week later the water had receded

Flood, 1894, West 2nd Place, at Mill Creek RJ

1894 Flood.   WCPA

enough so that businessmen could get into their storerooms to clear mud and debris. Linda Klindt stated that at Klindt's Bookstore on Second Street, *"we still find sand from this flood behind the radiators"*. The high-water mark has been indicated on several buildings downtown, including Klindt's Bookstore (which was the Nickelsen Bookstore at that time). Philip Klindt recalled, *"My great-grandmother, Belle Cooper Rinehart, told the story of promising her five-year old son that he could build a boat when the flood waters reached the bottom of the steps leading to their house, which later became The Dalles Hospital, on the bluff above Fourth Street. One morning, to her amazement she heard the sound of hammering; her son was starting to build his boat!"*

"The bluff was reached in places this season, and may have been in earlier years; but there is evidence that the highest water known for a long time was experienced in 1894. In the Columbia River are several islands which the Indians have used

Another flood   WCPA

1894 Flood, 9th Street Bridge

WCPA

2nd Street, 1894 flood   DM

for the sepulcure of their dead for ages past, and these have been washed over during this flood. If this had happened previously the bleached bones of chiefs and warriors would not have been found - as they have been ever since white men inhabited this region - to show the action of the elements for many decades. All former high water marks are obliterated, and the one for 1894 will stand out prominently in the future."[5]

The flood of 1948 was the last great flood on the Columbia with the water reaching the west end of Second Street by the Chamber of Commerce and the old St. Mary's Academy playground and entered basements along Second Street. The flood peaked in mid-June 1948. This flood caused great destruction along the Columbia, destroying Vanport which was a large housing community in North Portland.

As the big dams were built they provided flood control; many of the old flood plains have now been built upon, including much of the Port of The Dalles. The Georgie Burton, the last of the Columbia River steamships, had been brought to the canal to be restored. The 1948 flood water raised the steamboat and when it receded the ship was straddling the side of the canal and broke into pieces.

The Dalles is a great fruit country but it didn't fare so well on September 28, 1949, when the great Pineapple War took place. There was a Longshoreman's strike on the Pacific Coast, but the Port of The Dalles said they could unload a

Philip and Paul Klindt, 1948 flood, Klindt farm.   PK

shipment of Dole Pineapple here anyway. So, the Dole Company sent the ship up the Columbia to The Dalles where it would be unloaded at the Port by the Teamsters, but the Longshoremen in Portland found out and sent a group of Longshoremen to The Dalles to halt the unloading. Once the Longshoremen arrived in The Dalles there was a confrontation between the two groups. Several people were slightly injured in the melee that day and lots of pineapple made its way into the Columbia River. The site of the great Pineapple War was at the Port dock which was at the foot of Union Street. Until recent years, the pilings of the old Port could still be seen.

Rushing waters   WCHM

Fishing at Celilo   WCPA

The Dalles Dam was built in the 1950s and it was dedicated in 1959, by then Vice President Richard M. Nixon. Besides electricity, the dams were built for navigation, irrigation, flood control and recreation. Unfortunately, The Dalles Dam created a lake which covered Celilo Canal and Celilo Falls in 1957, a great resource to the Indian economy and culture and one of the great natural wonders of the United States.

In 1964, the whole northwest experienced an unusual combination of frozen ground, heavy snowfall followed by a warming rain. The result was extensive damage to roads, bridges and property throughout Washington, Oregon and northern California. In 1996, upper Mill Creek flooded, causing blockage at the tunnel to the river causing water to backup in the storm drainage system, and flooding many businesses in the downtown. Although these floods were severe, they were not as devastating as those floods prior to the installation of the dams.

2nd Explosion before the flooding of the falls, during the dam construction.   WCPA

The river was the main means of transportation until the coming of the railroad and highways. At that time the city was cut off from the river except for commercial transportation by barge. Beginning in the 1980s, the people began to think of the river as a recreation area, spurred on by windsurfing. The Dalles began to look for ways to reconnect to the river.

The Dalles Dam. Dedicated, 1959   WCPA

Underpass reconnecting the town to the river at the end of Union St.   WJ

Building the new underpass allowed for that connection. A ten mile walking/cycling trail extends from the Columbia Gorge Discovery Center and Wasco County Historical Museum to The Dalles Dam.

Riverfront Trail is a 10 mile hiking/biking path running east to west along the Columbia River   CW

1   Wm. H. McNeal, *History of Wasco County Oregon,* (The Dalles, OR: self published, 1953) p. 202.

2   Lockley, p. 279.

3   Shaver, p. 141.

4   Ibid., p. 142.

5   Ibid., p. 146.

14

TRAILS TO ROADS

Because of the prime location of The Dalles on the Columbia River, the main transportation route of the inland Northwest, the town grew into a major supply and distribution center. When gold was discovered in eastern Oregon and Idaho, the need to transfer supplies and freight from water to land gave rise to warehousing and wholesale businesses. Since none of the rivers which flow into the Columbia from central and eastern Oregon are commercially

1899. Freight teams in Antelope en route from The Dalles to Prineville   LCD

navigable, The Dalles became the embarkation point for stage and freight lines leading south and east, starting in the early 1860s. And when central Oregon began to be settled in the 1880s and 1890s, large numbers of sheep, cattle, and hogs would be driven to The Dalles, to the stockyards of H. E. Saltmarsh on the east end of town, to be loaded onto trains or boats for Portland or the Puget Sound markets.

As early as 1863, there was through stagecoach service from The Dalles to Boise and Salt Lake City, operating via the Oregon Trail route and La Grande. The stage ran three times a week during the first year, and increased to daily service by 1864. Fare from The Dalles to Salt Lake City was $240 - no small sum. A second through route went from The Dalles to Canyon City, operated by the Pony Express after 1862. This route was also extended to Boise and Salt Lake city a few years later, and ran three times a week.

Early wagon routes, 1884   DUE, JOHN

Stagecoach   WCHM

Bakeoven stage station en route to Canyon City.   WCPA

In addition to stagecoach service south and southeast, there was stagecoach service along the Oregon Trail route, extending to Wallula and Walla Walla, which sped up when a road was constructed along the old wagon route on the south bank of the Columbia to Wallula in 1867. The stagecoaches also carried the mail, an important contract for many of the stagecoach enterprises, since on many routes there was not enough passenger traffic to support the line.

After the decline of the gold mines, service south of The Dalles went to Prineville, the main center of Central Oregon. The stage was established in 1872, and left The Dalles on Mondays, taking three days to reach Prineville. Eventually this became the major route to Canyon City via a connecting route. Later service was extended to six times a week, starting from The Dalles every day except Sunday. According to John Due,*"The stage companies required watering stations about every 12 miles, and inns for overnight stays about every 50 miles."* [1]

Stage at Antelope Hotel   WCPA

In the late 1800s: *"the stage left the Umatilla House, at Union and First Streets in The Dalles, at 7 a.m. First came the steep climb up Brewery Grade, down to Three mile, up again and over the second ridge, and down to Five mile, and then the same process to Eight Mile, along much the same route as the present U.S. 197.*

Eight Mile House…was the first regular stop for horses and the passengers. Then came a much longer climb up Ward's Hill and down into the valley of Fifteen mile, to the stop, after 1882, at the Eleven Mile House, later called Boyd. In earlier years the stop was at old Wasco or Boyd, where an inn had been built in 1868. Boyd replaced Wasco and the latter vanished.

At the site of old Wasco, the stage turned south to go up the Long Hollow road, parting company with the state route…A long steady climb up Long Hollow replaced the roller coaster road north of Boyd, and a stop was made at Nansene, five miles up the Hollow, where Thomas Ward had built an inn….Five miles up another stop for watering the horses was made at Chicken Springs. The last two miles involved a long pull over Tygh Ridge, and then the precipitous drop to the Deschutes and the inn at Sherar's.

Sherar's was the first major stop, with a late lunch for the passengers… and then the horses were changed… After the river was crossed at Sherar's bridge, the afternoon was one of continuous climbing from 700 feet at the bridge to about 3,000 feet at the summit. The route followed Buck Hollow….to Bakeoven, the end of the day's run. The inn, build by Andre Smith in 1872, was located in a draw just off the main ridge….

Wards Mill. 1900's.　　　　　　　　　　　　　　　　　　　　　　　WCPA

The stages did not run overnight. The passengers had dinner, spent the night, and were off early the next morning, the Prineville stage heading south down steep and formidable Cow Canyon, on a 2,000 foot drop, the Canyon City stage eastward down through Cross Hollows, Antelope and Burnt Ranch and along the river to Canyon City."[2]

The earliest roads were informally built, coming into existence by repeated use and casual work done by the travelers themselves. *"Virtually every caravan and every freighter carried picks and shovels and contributed to the elementary road improvement… Few of these roads ran straight for any distance, unlike those in the Midwest, instead winding and curving with the terrain."[3]*

But some areas were too rugged for such casual efforts, and people sought aid from the Federal government; this came in the form of wagon road grants.

The most famous in this area was that awarded to The Dalles Military Road Company. The gold rush to Canyon City in 1862 and the following years stimulated businessmen in The Dalles to form The Dalles and Boise Road Company in order to increase trade with both Canyon City and Idaho. They built a road, of sorts, from Cross Hollows (near Shaniko) to the John Day River and on to Canyon City. Later it was extended to Boise. But finances were a problem, and the contractors seized the company. However, with the possibility of acquiring land grants, a new company formed, including some of the original stockholders, the contractors of the original road, their lawyers, and others. The new company bought the Gordon Bridge over the Deschutes, and did a nominal amount of work on already existing roads, and in 1869, the governor certified that the road had been completed, thus awarding the company *"some 685,440 acres. For 357 miles of road; it was estimated later that the company had spent perhaps no more than $6,000 in total on the road - which was already built."* [4]

This road crossed into Sherman County at Gordon Bridge, three miles south of the mouth of the Deschutes, passed west of Wasco and Moro, through Grass Valley, and on south to Cross Hollows. The land grant gave the company alternate sections of land in a band three miles wide on either side of the roads; if land had already been taken up within this band, the company could choose

Paving east end of 2nd Street   DM

sections from within a 10 mile limit, thus covering a major portion of the western part of Sherman County. This land became unavailable for homesteading. Even though the company announced it would sell the land at the government homestead price, $1.25 an acre, there were few takers. In 1876, the entire land grant was sold to

Early West 6th Street   WCHM

Edward Martin for $125,000. It was eventually sold off by his heirs, who had formed the Eastern Oregon Land Company, but not without numerous legal battles over the years.

However, as soon as The Dalles Military Road Company received the land grant, it discontinued all maintenance work on the road; the Gordon Bridge, already in poor shape, fell into the river. The remainder of the road reverted to local use and maintenance.

Eventually, with the demise of the gold mines and the increased settlement of Central Oregon, the road south of The Dalles, became a major route. The route stayed west of the Deschutes River to Tygh Valley, and crossed the Deschutes below the falls, north of the mouth of the White River, at Sherars Bridge.

From The Dalles west, the highway to Portland came later. In the 1870's, the Oregon legislature appropriated funds to build a wagon road from the mouth of the Sandy River through to The Dalles. According to Lockley, *"The road,*

Ferryboat from Union St. in The Dalles to the Washington shore.   DM

if road it could be called, was narrow, full of sharp curves and the grades were so steep that it was often necessary to double teams to pull up the hill. In the winter the road was often impassable, on account of the deep mud. However, it was an improvement on the old trail used by the emigrants."[5]

It was not until 1912 that Samuel Hill, son-in-law of James J. Hill, the Empire Builder and president of the Great Northern Railroad, conceived the idea of building a highway along the south bank of the Columbia River. An ardent advocate of Good Roads, a world traveler who was comfortable in the company of both wealth and royalty, Hill enlisted the cooperation of Simon Benson, a millionaire lumberman of Portland, and John B. Yeon, another wealthy, public spirited citizen of Portland, as well as others. He believed that the highway should be built in the best possible manner, and took with him to Europe, Samuel Lancaster and other engineers to study the roads of Switzerland, Italy, France and elsewhere. Lancaster was appointed consulting engineer of the Columbia River Highway project, and using the engineering knowledge he had gained in Europe, supervised all the preliminary construction work, including the determination of the route so that there would be no grade of more than 5%. The reinforced concrete bridges and viaducts were designed, "*in each case to fit the structure into its natural setting and to make the completed bridge a work of art as well as an example of the best economical engineer practice.*"[6]

Rowena Loops under construction, 1913-1922.   WCPA

Completed Rowena Loops   WCPA

The Columbia River Highway opened with great ceremony in August, 1915. By 1921, The Dalles had a land link with Portland that was not dependent on

1913 Highway Dedication   DM

Multnomah Falls, 840' high, on the Columbia River Highway   DM

someone else's scheduling and pricing. And with the rapidly growing popularity of the motor-car, a new era began.

Traveling on "the old highway" as it is now called, was slow, since, in order to meet the requirement of maximum 5% grade, the road was built with a great number of curves: from Crown Point down to the river, a drop of 600 feet, *"it was necessary to have the road form a figure eight paralleling itself five times."*[7] And between Hood River and The Dalles, the road had to climb over the bluffs which had hindered land traffic over the Cascades. The twisting Rowena Loops effectively slowed traffic to a few miles per hour. The average drive to Portland would take about 3 ½ hours. Highway 30 was replaced by a divided freeway in the 1950s and 60s; known now as I-84, and takes about 1 ½ hours to reach Portland. As Highway 30 (aka U.S. 30) was replaced by the river level highway, parts of the original Highway 30 were destroyed. In the 1980s, efforts began to restore the old highway to a biking and hiking route. During the 1990s to the present, much of this work has been completed including restoring the Twin Tunnels west of Mosier, Oregon.

Climbing Columbia River Highway   WCPA

Mitchell Point Tunnel. Destroyed when I-84 was built   VW

View from Rowena Crest   WJ

The section from Troutdale, Oregon, to The Dalles, Oregon, received Historical Landmark status in 2000 and is known as the Historic Columbia River Highway. Much of the original rockwork can be seen on the east and west ends of the highway.

The Rowena Crest viewpoint, at the top of the Rowena Loops, provides a panoramic view of the Columbia River Gorge and the curves in the old highway. The Tom McCall Wildflower Preserve at Rowena Crest is an excellent location for viewing wildflowers.

1   Due, p. 52.

2   Ibid., pp. 52-53.

3   Ibid., p. 35.

4   Ibid., p. 38.

5   Lockley, Vol. I, p. 831.

6   Ibid., p. 838.

7   Ibid., p. 834.

15

THE COMING OF THE RAILROADS

The history of the railroads along the Columbia is a complex, confusing story of competing companies, personal rivalries, financial problems, corporate reorganizations, and overlapping interests.

The first serious interest in promoting a transcontinental railroad to the Northwest came in 1845, when a proposal was made to build a railroad from Lake Michigan to the Oregon coast, to encourage trade with the Orient.[1] However, the boundary dispute with England and the discovery of gold in California made California a more obvious goal. The Union Pacific received a large land grant, as well as government loans to encourage construction, and built a rail line westward from Missouri. The Central Pacific, with similar funding, built a line east from Sacramento. They met at Promontory, Utah, on May 10, 1869, where the last spike was driven.

Steam train west of The Dalles   JW

Despite the difficulty of finding a buildable route, The Northern Pacific still sought to build a railway to Puget Sound with a branch down the Columbia to Portland. However, funding was a major problem also. Although it was awarded land grants, other government financial assistance was denied. Bank financing was arranged, but construction of the line happened in fits and starts in the 1870s.

Meanwhile, Henry Villard, one of the major entrepreneurs of the last three decades of the nineteenth century, came into the picture. He became involved with Portland businessmen who wanted to build a direct line to the east. He acquired the Oregon Steam Navigation Company, merged it with the new Oregon Railway and Navigation Company, and finally got control of the

Early train & track.   WCHM

Train west of The Dalles.   JW

Northern Pacific in 1881, with the goal of forcing it to come to Portland. At the same time, he built eastward from The Dalles to Wallula, incorporating the old portage line around Celilo Falls, and connecting with the local railroad to Walla Walla. Late in 1881, rail construction started westward from The Dalles, reaching Portland in August 1883. The line connected with the Northern Pacific at Wallula in 1883 and with the Union Pacific via the Oregon Short Line through Idaho in 1884. Thus, within only a few years, Portland and The Dalles had two routes to the east. Union Pacific acquired full control over the line south of the Columbia in 1889. In 1909, James J. Hill, who had acquired the Northern Pacific eight years earlier, built the Spokane, Portland and Seattle line along the north bank of the Columbia. Because of the rivalry between the Union Pacific and the Northern Pacific, or perhaps more precisely, the rivalry between their chief executives James J. Hill and Edward Harriman, competing rail lines were built south along both banks of the Deschutes River in the same year. The Northern Pacific line still runs to Bend along the Deschutes, crossing the river and over the east-west Union Pacific tracks near Celilo.

Many of the laborers who worked for the railway were of Asian decent. The Chinese came as early as the 1860s to search for gold in the John Day country. When the gold ran out, many stayed and helped to build the railroad, and later worked in the salmon cannery. The Japanese came in the 1890s to work primarily on the branch railroads. Many of them stayed on and became farmers.

Sternwheeler hauling wagons.   WCHM

With the coming of the railroad, river traffic on the upper Columbia virtually disappeared, since the railroad had taken over the portage railway. The Dalles businessmen, whose business was closely connected with river traffic, pushed for the completion of the locks at the Cascades. They also founded a steamship line, popularly known as the Regulator Line to regulate freight rates in competition with the railroad's virtual monopoly in hauling freight along the Columbia. The opening of the locks gave a breath of new life to river traffic, and the scenic trip even attracted many train passengers who would break their long distance journey at The Dalles to board the steamers for the rest of the trip to Portland. The steamer, *Bailey Gatzert,* was brought from Puget Sound in 1901, and became a familiar sight along the river, making a daily round trip

The Dalles Train Depot was located at the end of Liberty Street, north of 2nd Street.   DM

Railroad yard and roundhouse east of The Dalles   WCPA

from Portland to The Dalles for over a decade. It retained much of the elegance of the earlier Columbia River steamers.

In the first years, the railroad could not handle the volume of freight, especially during harvest season, and in 1905 the state built a portage railway around Celilo, later extended to The Dalles, to aid transfer of water freight. In 1915 the Celilo Canal and locks were completed with the hope that business from upper river ports would be revived.

Unfortunately, it was too late. The railroads, now financially much stronger, simply lowered their freight rates. The opening of the Columbia River Highway the same year also cut into the steamships' business. By 1920, the traffic through the canal was virtually non-existent. The last stern-wheeler left The Dalles in 1923, and when river transport revived in the 1930s, barges became the main means of transporting freight.

100 new box cars along the Columbia River   WCPA

1   Peter J. Lewty, *To the Columbia Gateway: The Oregon Railway and the Northern Pacific, 1879-1884,*
     (Pullman, WA: Washington State University Press, 1987), p.1.

16

20th TO 21st CENTURY

In the 1980s, The Dalles achieved a first; it was the first city in the U.S. to have a terrorist attack. *"In 1981, followers of the Bhagwan Shree (meaning "Sir God" in Sanskrit) Rajneesh, had paid $5.75 million for a remote sixty-four thousand-acre ranch in Wasco County, a two hour drive from The Dalles, the county seat. Their*

Bhagwan Shree Rajneesh   THE DALLES CHRONICLE

plan was to build a "Buddhafield," an agricultural commune in which they celebrate their "enlightened master's" credo of beauty, love, and guiltless sex."[1] The followers were very visible because of their red, orange and maroon attire.

Eventually several thousand followers were living on the ranch where they built an extensive number of buildings and greenhouses. Since The Dalles is the county seat of Wasco County, they came often and challenged the state land use laws. The Rajneesh poisoned several salad bars in The Dalles and sickened between 600-700 people. They attempted to gain control of the county by importing hundreds of homeless from large cities, to influence the county elections. Federal charges were brought against some of the leaders of the group because of their open threats to state and local officials and they were jailed as a result of those actions. As their internal distrust and paranoia grew,

Plaque on flagpole at post office in Antelope, OR   MM
'Dedicated to those of this community who throughout the Rajneesh invasion and occupation of 1981 - 1985 remained,
resisted and remembered...'"The only thing necessary for the triumph of evil is for good men to do nothing" (Edmund Burke)'

the ranch fell apart and, because of immigration violations, the Bhagwan was arrested while trying to flee the country by private plane. After the dissolution of the commune, The Muddy Ranch, near Antelope, then became a Young Life camp, a non-denominational camp for teens.

The Dalles has proved fortunate to have several economic bases; tourism, industry and agriculture. The Dalles airport, at Dallesport, Washington, was established in 1931. It was used as a training field during WWII and now is a regional airport. The aluminum plant was a primary employer from the 1950s to 2000. Significant new industries are Google and wind power generation.

There is a wealth of historical buildings, murals, museums and sites to visit in The Dalles and surrounding areas, many with landmark status.

The Dalles Commercial Historic District was listed in the National Register of Historic Places in 1986. The Trevitt's Addition Historic District, located northwest of The Dalles Commercial Historic District, was determined eligible for listing in the National Register in 1987. The following photos are of existing buildings, many of which are part of the historic districts listed above.

St. Paul's Church, 1875 and rectory, 1885 at 601 Union St. WCPA

Boca Beer Depot, now the Baldwin Saloon at 1st and Court Streets.   DM

Indian Shaker Church, built 1890's. View from the exterior only, at The Shilo Inn, Junction I-84 and U.S. 197.   WJ

Building the post office in 1917 at 2nd and Union Streets.   DM

U.S. Post Office, now AmeriTitle, at 2nd and Union Streets; and the 2nd county courthouse, built in 1881, now the Clock Tower Ales at 3rd and Court Streets.   DM

3rd Wasco County Courthouse, built in 1914, 5th and WashingtonStreets.   DM

Sunshine Flour Mill, built in 1908, now the Sunshine Mill Artisan Plaza and Winery at 901 East 2nd Street.   DM

City Hall built in 1908, included the fire station. The fire station is now a fire museum at 313 Court Street.

DM

Building of the Granada Theater, completed in 1929, as the first talking movie
house west of the Mississippi at 2nd and Washington Streets.   DM

Bank building at 3rd and Washington Streets. Photo shows the Vogt Fountain, built in 1911, which now sits in the rose garden at the entrance of Sorosis Park on Scenic Drive. DM

Depot for the Great Southern Railroad to Dufur, built in 1912, now Cannon Packer Gift Shop at 1006 East 2nd Street. DM

Eastern Oregon T.B. Hospital, built in 1929, adjacent to Sorosis Park, now the administration building for Columbia Gorge Community College.   DM

Civic Auditorium, built in 1921, as a tribute to the veterans, located at 323 East 4th Street.   WJ

Carnegie Library built in 1910, now The Dalles Art Center at 220 East 4th Street.   WJ

In 1986, Congress established the Columbia Gorge National Scenic Area Act which created a scenic area from the Sandy River, near Portland, to the Deschutes River east of The Dalles, excluding the incorporated cities. The results of that Act established the Skamania Lodge in Washington and The Columbia Gorge Discovery Center and Museum, west of The Dalles.

Wheat became the primary crop in the surrounding area due to deep soil, adequate rainfall, and moderate climate. For the same reasons, fruit orchards were planted. They became another profitable crop when irrigation from the river began in 1965, doubling the fruit production. The Dalles is now one of the main suppliers of fresh cherries on the international market and vineyards are the most recent addition.

Columbia Gorge Discovery Center and Wasco County Historical Museum, 3 miles west of The Dalles on Old Hwy. 30.   RP

111

Orchards around The Dalles   WCPA

Cherry harvest   WCPA

Wheat field in Wasco Co.   WCPA

Wheat threshing   WCHM

The Dalles has always been a primary service area for the entire region of North Central Oregon and South Central Washington. Originally Native Americans gathered and traded on the river and later, pioneers established the city and offered services to other travelers.

The Dalles (Win-Quatt) continues, as it always has, to be a center of commerce - recognized for its location, beauty and history.

Fishing Platform of Thomas William Mosqueda, 2011.   CW

---

1   Judith Miller, Stephen Engelberg, & Wm. Broad. *Germs: Biological Weapons and America's Secret War,* (NY: Simon & Schuster, 2001), p. 15.

ABOUT THE AUTHORS

It is nearly impossible to describe Philip and Linda Klindt. They were bohemians at heart; free thinkers and all inclusive. Individually they were brilliant, and as a couple they shared great passions for history, travel and people. They were inspiring and compassionate, with great senses of humor. There seemed no need for them to distinguish between family, friends or new acquaintances. They had no children of their own, yet, "adopted" several and mentored many more.

Philip Klindt was born and raised on the Columbia River in The Dalles, Oregon. His father was a farmer and his mother, a teacher. Linda Roubalik was from a rural town in Minnesota. They met in the 1960s at the University of Washington in the Russian Language Program, eventually marrying and renting an apartment close to the campus. Dedicated students and friends met at their home nightly to eat, drink and discuss the great philosophers and present day events.

After Linda received her Masters and Philip his Ph.D., they moved to Austin, Texas where he taught at the University. Linda taught at the University of Virginia while pursuing her doctorate. It was also in the 1960s that they began guiding tours to Russia. They later broadened those tours to include most of Europe. In the early years, when the trips were geared toward their students, they camped with Volkswagen buses. As their success in tours increased, their accommodations were upgraded to three star hotels. Each trip was meticulously planned, with Linda doing research and creating booklets for each traveler.

In 1981, they moved back to The Dalles to purchase the historic bookstore on the main street of town. The Weigelt Bookstore, as it was known then, had been established in 1870, by the Nickelsen Brothers, and the Klindts would be only the third family to own the business. One of the stipulations that came with the purchase was that one of the previous owners, Ms. Edna Weigelt, would continue to assist at the store for at least a year. Edna worked there another 20 years, retiring at age 91. Klindt's Booksellers is presently the oldest, continuously operated, bookstore in the state of Oregon.

Philip and Linda made few physical changes to the bookstore. They appreciated the "feel" of the building. The wooden floors remain to this day as they were in the 1800s. Some of the display cases and much of the side shelving has been retained. Many famous and infamous people have wandered through the store, stopping to chat with locals and to visit with ghosts of the past.

In 1985, the Klindts added a second store, renting an enclosed pass-through, between 1st and 2nd streets, which they turned into a unique retail space. They kept the doors open from early morning till night, 7 days a week, giving access for people to enter the downtown core area through the walkway. There you could find gifts from other countries, local art and the ever popular, rubber chickens. For 15 years this space also served as an open forum for the general public. Coffee and donuts were offered daily and many heated discussions and much laughter were had around the small wooden tables inside the store.

Linda had always wanted a used bookstore, and so, in 1989, they expanded again, renting a building two doors east of the main bookstore. There she opened a combination, rare book/antique/ice cream shop. Linda and Philip both spoke several languages and had a great affinity for foreign cinema. With this 3rd store they had a little extra room, so they began collecting and renting those movies and by 1999 they had accumulated an inventory of over 3,000 foreign and U.S. art films.

The Klindts were the town historians and greeters and their stores served as information centers. At times the front doors were so covered with event posters that you could scarcely see inside. If a visitor from out of town had an interest in the local history, it was not unusual for Philip to pack them into his van and take them on a mini tour of the area. They were active community members, serving on numerous boards and were often called on for speaking engagements. Philip was a regular on a local radio talk show.

The bookstore worked closely with the schools and library, establishing many reading programs and contests to inspire children to read. The Klindts encouraged people of all ages to travel. They took the time to explain their views of different countries and were always interested in the stories people had to tell upon return from their own journeys.

Linda and Philip were both excellent cooks and, reminiscent of their college days, they fixed wonderful dinners six nights a week, encouraging multi-generational family members and friends to join them at their table; usually 8-15 people per night. The only exception to the home dinners was on Thursday nights, when 20-30 people would meet at the Sugar Bowl, a local pub/restaurant, where they would spend hours eating, drinking and discussing local issues and world events. The Sugar Bowl, established around 1932, is one of the oldest eateries in town. Klindts had their own table.

Linda passed away in 2000, and Philip in 2010. Their family rented the largest room in town for their memorial services. The room held, by law, about 600 people. Both memorials were filled to capacity, actually utilizing the gymnasium below for the overflow crowds; a testament to the type of people they were.

Consummate educators and continuous givers, it is appropriate then, that this history book would be their final gift to the community. Proceeds from the sale of this edition will go back to The Columbia Gorge Discovery Center & Wasco County Historical Museum to help with other regional publications.

Klindt's Booksellers is now owned by Philip and Linda's nieces and nephews, Dane & Stephanie Klindt and Kristin Klindt-Perez & Joaquin Perez.

Widge Johnson and Carolyn Wood

1890's photo showing Nickelsens bookstore.   JW

Nickelsen brothers, 1st owners of bookstore, 1800's.   WCPA

Paul, Edna & Gus Weigelt, 2nd owners of bookstore. 1927-1981.   PK

Linda and Philip Klindt, 3rd owners of bookstore, 1981.   PK

Klindt's Booksellers, 2011. 315 East 2nd, The Dalles, Oregon   CW

WIN – QUATT

BIBLIOGRAPHY

Allen, John Eliot. *The Magnificent Gateway: A Geology of the Columbia River Gorge.* Forest Grove, OR: Timber Press, Incorporated, July 1, 1979.

Biddle, Nicholas. *The Journals of the Expedition Under the Command of Capts. Lewis and Clark.* New York, NY: Heritage Press, 1962.

Binns, Archie. *Peter Skene Ogden: Fur Trader.* Portland, OR: Binford & Mort Publishing. 1967.

Due, John Fitzgerald. *Roads and Rails South from Columbia.* Bend, OR: Maverick Publications, 1991.

Eels, Myron. *Hymns in the Chinook Jargon Language.* Portland, OR: Geo. H. Himes Publishing House. 1898.

Farnham, Thomas Jefferson. *Life, Adventures, and Travels in California, To Which are Added the Conquest of California, Travels in Oregon, and History of the Gold Regions.* New York, NY: Cornish, Lamport & Co., 1850.

Farnham, Thomas Jefferson. *1839 Wagon Train Journal: Travels in the Great Western Prairies.....and the Oregon Territory.* Monroe, OR. Northwest Interpretive Assoc. 1983.

Ferguson-McKeown, Martha. Historic Umatilla House at The Dalles, *Oregon Historical Quarterly,* Vol. 31, pg 37-41. Salem, OR: Statesman Publishing Co., 1930.

Fremont, John C. and Torrey, John and Hall, James. *Report of the Exploring Expedition to the Rocky Mountains, Document #166.* Blair & Rives, 1845.

French, Giles. *The Golden Land: A History of Sherman County, Oregon.* Portland, OR, Oregon Historical Society, 1958

Fuller-Victor, Frances. *The Early Indian Wars of Oregon: Compiled from the Oregon Archives and Other Original Sources : with Muster Rolls.* Salem, OR: F.C. Baker, 1894.

Gray, William Henry. *A History of Oregon 1792-1849.* San Francisco: Bancroft, 1870.

Greer, Theodore Thurston. *Fifty Years in Oregon; Experiences, Observations and Commentaries.* New York, NY: Neale Publishing, 1912.

Johansen, Dorothy O. *Empire of the Columbia.* New York, NY: Harper and Row, 1956.

Knuth, Pricilla. *Picturesque Frontier: The Army's Fort Dalles.* Portland, OR: Oregon Historical Society Press. Dec., 1987.

Laughlin-Lord, Elizabeth. *Reminiscences of Eastern Oregon.* Portland, OR: Irwin-Hodson, 1903.

Lavender, David. *Westward Vision: The Story of the Oregon Trail.* Lincoln: University of Nebraska Press, 1963.

Lewty, Peter J. *To the Columbia Gateway: The Oregon Railway and the Northern Pacific, 1879-1884.* Pullman, WA: Washington State University Press, 1987.

Lockley, Fred. *History of the Columbia River Valley From The Dalles to the Sea.* Vol. I, II, and III. Chicago, IL: S. J. Clarke Publishing Co., 1928.

Lyman, Horace. *History of Oregon; the Growth of an American State,* Vol. II. NY: North Pacific Pub. Society, 1903.

Lyman, William Denison. *The Columbia River; Its History, Its Myths, Its Scenery, Its Commerce.* 4th Ed. Portland, OR: Binfords & Mort, 1963.

McNeal, William H. *History of Wasco County Oregon.* The Dalles, OR: Self published, 1953.

McNeal, William. *Some Historical Notes on Wasco County, Oregon Historical Quarterly,* Vol. 56, pg 81-85. Portland, OR: Abbott, Kerns & Bell, 1955.

Miller, Judith and Engelberg, Stephen and Broad, William. *Germs: Biological Weapons and America's Secret war.* NY: Simon & Schuster. 2001.

Mills, Randall V. *Stern-Wheelers Up Columbia: A Century of Steamboating in the Oregon Country.* Palo Alto, CA: Pacific Books, 1947.

Montgomery, Donna Wojcik. *Brazen Overlanders of 1845.* Maryland: Heritage Books, Revised edition, 1992.

Nesmith, James W. In a speech to the Oregon Pioneer Association in 1875, *"History of the Great Migration of 1843,"*http://www.oregon.gov/ODOT/CS/SSB/Oregon_Trail.shtml" 13 August 2011.

Parker, Rev., Samuel. *Journal of an Exploring Tour Beyond The Rocky Mountains.* Hudson, WI: Ross & Haines, 1967.

Ruby, Robert H. and Brown, John A. *Ferryboats on the Columbia River.* Seattle, WA: Superior Publishing Co., 1974.

Scaglione, John, Editor. *Ogdens Report of his 1829-30 Expedition.* California Historical Society, 1949.

Shaver, F.A. in collaboration with Rose, Arthur P. and Steele, R.F., and Adams A.F. *History of Central Oregon Embracing Wasco, Sherman, Gilliam, Wheeler, Crook, Lake and Klamath Counties.* Spokane, WA: Western Historical Publishing Company., 1905.

Sheller, Roscoe. *Ben Snipes Northwest Cattle King.* Portland, OR: Binfort & Mort, 1957.

Sheller, Roscoe. *The name was Olney.* Yakima, WA: Franklin Press, 1965.

Sullivan, John. "Annexation", *United States Magazine and Democratic Review 17, no.1* (July-August 1845): pg 5-10. NY, Langley

Teiser, Sidney. Cyrus Olney, Associate Justice of Oregon Territory Supreme Court. *Oregon Historical Quarterly,* Vol. 64, pg 309-322. Portland, OR: Abbot, Kerns & Bell, 1963.

Wilkes, Commander. *Narrative of the United States Exploring Expedition, During the Years 1838, 1839, 1840, 1841, 1842.* NY: G. P. Putnam & Co., 1856.

Wyeth, Nathaniel Journals of Captain Nathaniel J. *Wyeth's Expedition to the Oregon Country, 1831-1836.* Fairfiled, WA:Ye Galleon Press, 1985.

Young, Fredrick George, Editor. Jason Lee's Diary. *Historical Quarterly,* Vol. 16, No.1. Portland, OR: Oregon March, 1915.

The Barlow Road, Clackamas County Historical Society and Wasco County Historical Society, J.Y. Hollingsworth Co., Portland, OR, 1991.

The Way of the Inland Empire. *The Dalles Times Mountaineer.* Jan. 1, 1889, p 1.

Wiped Out By Fire. *The Dalles Times Mountaineer.* Sept. 3, 1891. p 1.

ADDITIONAL RESOURCES

Ambrose, Stephen E. *Undaunted Courage.* NY: Simon Schuster, 1996.

Attwell, Jim. *Columbia River Gorge History, Vol. I and Vol. II.* Skamania, WA: Tahlkie Books, 1974-1975.

Bancroft, Hubert H. *Bancroft's Works, Vol. I History of Oregon 1834-48; Vol. II History of Oregon 1848-1888.* San Francisco, CA: History Company, 1888.

Bullard, Oral. *Lancaster's Road: The Historic Columbia River Scenic Highway.* Beaverton, OR: TMS Book Service, 1982.

Burkhardt, D.C. Jesse. *Railroads of the Columbia River Gorge.* San Francisco, CA: Arcadia Publishing 2004.

Campbell, Art H. *Antelope, the Saga of a Western Town.* Bend, OR; Maverick Publications, 1990.

Coffman, Lloyd W. *Blazing a Wagon Trail to Oregon: A Weekly Chronicle of the Great Migration of 1843.* Enterprise, OR: Echo Books, 1993.

Donaldson, Ivan J.; Cramer, Fritz. *Fishwheels on the Columbia.* Portland, OR: Binford & Mort, 1971.

French, Giles. *Cattle Company of Pete French.* Portland, OR: Binford & Mort, 1964.

Gaston, Joseph, *Centennial History of Oregon 1811-1911. Vol I and Vol. II.* Chicago, IL: S. J. Clarke. 1912.

Hafen, Leroy R. and Ann W. *To the Rockies and Oregon 1839-1842. With Diaries and Accounts by Sidney Smith, Amos Cook, Joseph Holman, E. Willard Smith, Francis Fletcher, Joseph Williams, Obadiah Oakley, Robert Shortess, T.J. Farnham.* Glendale, CA: Arthur H Clark Company, 1960.

Holbrook, Stewart. *The Columbia.* NY: Rinehart & Co., 1956.

Jolley, Russ. *Wildflowers of the Columbia River Gorge.* Portland, OR: Oregon Historical Society Press. 1988.

Lambert Wood, Elizabeth. *Pete French – Cattle King.* Portland, OR: Binford & Mort, 1951.

Lancaster, Samuel Christopher. *The Columbia America's Great Highway Through the Cascades Mountains To the Sea.* Portland, OR, 1915.

Lundell, John. *Governmental History of Wasco County Oregon.* Published by author, 1970.

Lundell, John H. *History of School Districts & School Houses Wasco County, Oregon.* Wasco County Historical Press, The Dalles, OR., 2009.

McArthur, Lewis A. *Oregon Geographic Names,* 3rd Ed.. Oregon Historical Society Portland, OR: Binford & Mort. 1952.

Roberts, Wilma. *Celilo Falls: Remembering Thunder.* The Dalles, OR: Wasco County Historical Museum Press., 1997.

Seufert, Francis. *Wheels of Fortune.* Oregon Historical Society, Portland, OR: 1980

Timmon, Fritz. *Blow for the Landing a 100 Years of Steam Navigation on the Waters of the West.* Caldwell, ID: Caxton Printers. 1973.

Ward Zopf, Nancy. *Dallesport, Washington: The Paris of the West.* The Dalles, OR: Wasco County Historical Museum Press, 2008.

Ward Zopf, Nancy. *Hospitals of The Dalles.* The Dalles, OR: Wasco County Historical Museum Press., 2009.

Wyman, Mary Alice, Editor. *Selections from the Autobiography of Elizabeth Oakes Smith.* Lewiston Journal Company; 1st edition, 1924. NY: Columbia University Press.

NOTES AND REFLECTIONS